Zero Waste
in Business

Zero Waste in Business

Fergus O'Connell

Independent Book Publisher

Legend Business, 2 London Wall Buildings,
London EC2M 5UU
info@legend-paperbooks.co.uk
www.legendpress.co.uk

Contents © Fergus O'Connell 2011

The right of Fergus O'Connell to be identified as the author of
this work has been asserted by him in accordance with the
Copyright, Designs and Patent Act 1988.

British Library Cataloguing in Publication Data available.

ISBN 978-1-9077563-8-2

Set in Times

Printed by Lightning Source, Milton Keynes, UK

Cover designed by:
EA Digitial, Leicester
www.eadigital.com

Independent Book Publisher

Further works by Fergus O'Connell:

Earn More, Stress Less: How To Attract Wealth Using the Secret Science of Getting Rich

Work Less, Achieve More: Great Ideas to Get Your Life Back

Simply Brilliant – The Competitive Advantage of Common Sense, 3rd edition

How To Get More Done: Seven Days to Achieving More

Fast Projects: Project Management When Time Is Short

How To Do A Great Job – And Go Home On Time

Call The Swallow

How To Run Successful Projects – The Silver Bullet, 3rd edition

How To Run Successful Projects In Web-Time

How To Run Successful High-Tech Project-Based Organizations

About the Author

Fergus O'Connell is one of the world's leading authorities on project management and getting things done in the shortest possible time. *The Sunday Business Post* has described him as having 'more strings to his bow than a Stradivarius'. He has a First in Mathematical Physics and has worked in information technology, software development and general management.

Fergus has spent much of the last thirty years either doing, teaching, learning, writing or thinking about project management. In 1992, he founded ETP (www.etpint.com), which is now one of the world's leading programme and project management companies. His project management method – Structured Project Management/The Ten Steps – has influenced a generation of project managers. In 2003 this method was used to plan and execute the Special Olympics World Games, the world's biggest sporting event that year. His radical methods for shortening projects are in use by a growing band of devotees. His experience covers projects around the world; he has taught project management in Europe, North America, South America and Asia. He holds two patents.

Fergus is the author of twelve books, both fiction and non-fiction. The first of these, sometimes known simply as *The Silver Bullet* has become both a bestseller and a classic. *Simply Brilliant* – also a bestseller – was runner-up in the WHSmith Book Awards 2002. *Call The Swallow* was shortlisted for the 2002 Kerry Ingredients Irish Fiction Prize and nominated for the Hughes & Hughes/Sunday Independent Novel of the Year. His books have been translated into 20 languages.

Fergus has written on project management for *The Sunday Business Post, Computer Weekly* and *The Wall Street Journal*. He has lectured on project management at University College Cork, Trinity College Dublin, Bentley College, Boston University, the Michael Smurfit Graduate School of Business and on television for the National Technological University.

He has two children and lives on the south coast of France.

To contact Fergus, email: fergus.oconnell@wanadoo.fr

For Louise and Sue – true friends

'Perhaps when a man has special knowledge and special powers like my own, it rather encourages him to seek a complex explanation when a simpler one is at hand.'

Sherlock Holmes

CONTENTS

Preface

Imagine if you will, the following. You get a job managing a small car repair/servicing shop. The owner of the shop has been running it up until now but he wants to hire somebody who has had proper business and management training. That's you. There will be generous profit-sharing.

The shop employs two mechanics and there is a rule of thumb that each mechanic can service two cars a day. Obviously this is a rough rule – cars can take longer or shorter and sometimes big jobs have to be done which can last several days. But, in general, the two cars a day rule of thumb works pretty well. It even allows some time for those inevitable walk-in clients or emergencies. The owner tells you that the car repair shop is a relatively happy place to work and a fairly simple place to manage.

Now, as mentioned, you've come from a much more sophisticated organisation where people used to talk about "stretch goals" and "ambitious targets" and "aggressive schedules" and "tough challenges". And you decide that the car repair shop could benefit from these ideas. So you tell the two mechanics that you're going to "grow the business by 20% this year". You're also going to offer a new service where you will collect and return the client's car. The mechanics will do the collecting and returning. You tell them that this will enable them to "get closer to the customer".

So you do some marketing and, sure enough, business starts to increase. The mechanics get more overtime, the business makes more money and the customers get a better service. Everybody's happy.

Business continues to increase. But you don't want to hire any more mechanics to deal with the increased workload because that would increase costs and eat into your profits. So, instead, you tell the existing mechanics things like they'll "have to work smarter, not harder" and that if they don't do it, you'll find somebody who will, that they should be bringing you problems not solutions, they're not committed enough, and other useful advice like this.

The mechanics used to take a twenty minute tea break in the morning and afternoon (which often became half an hour) but with the increased pressure, they have to stop doing this. You're pleased about this because you never liked the idea much anyway. (Never mind that, as well as talking about football and girls and the weekend, the mechanics used to plan their work during these breaks and discuss technical problems.)

Now things start to go to hell a bit. Customers' cars aren't ready when promised. And since some customers tend to get more irate than others, these ones are given priority. But that means that you inevitably lose some who aren't happy with the service they are getting. And the mechanics complain because priorities are constantly changing. Back in the old days, when a car came in, a mechanic worked on it pretty much until it was done. Now, because of all the juggling of different jobs, the two mechanics are constantly switching from one priority to another. This adds further to the overload as, when they return to a particular car, they have to get their head back around the problem again, which takes additional time.

Because of the pressure to get cars picked up, worked on and delivered, mistakes are made. And so work is done which has to be re-done. And so there are more unhappy customers, refusing to pay for repairs or looking for discounts/refunds or saying that jobs are going to have to be re-done or taking their business elsewhere. And, of course, all of this loses you money.

And what used to be a happy place to work has become a place of great stress, long hours and unhappiness. Finally, one of the mechanics leaves and the word on the street is that this shop is not a place where people would want to work. Revenue may be up but profits are definitely down due to the waste caused by:

- no planning and resulting wasted effort;
- work being thrown away;
- re-work;
- switching between jobs.

And that's not even to mention loss of staff motivation and unhappy customers.

But, of course, you're a good manager. You would never preside over such a stupid scenario.

Instead, your organisation is probably like most organisations. At the beginning of the year, the owners, shareholders or board decide that they want to grow business as usual by, say, 15%. They also want to do some brand new things – new products, services, initiatives, take new directions. The management team takes this mission and launches a bunch of projects. Everybody in the organisation now has (a) maybe a day job and (b) almost certainly, a project-related workload. Most management teams expect everybody to undertake this workload. They say things like "that's just the culture here", "I don't want to hear anybody using the word 'can't'", "we like a can-do attitude here", "don't bring me problems, bring me solutions", "we're going to have to learn to do more with less" or – if somebody objects to all of this – "you're being inflexible", "not a team player" or (these days) "you're lucky to have a job". They also say things like "we don't have time to plan it, just go do it." And that is exactly what happens – projects and initiatives are either not planned properly or at all.

If the management team is a bit more enlightened it will tell people to schedule themselves, say, 70% for their day job and the remaining 30% for project work. While this is a great idea in theory, it almost never happens on the ground. And, anyway, how can somebody schedule themselves 70% for their day job if it's a full-time job? Not do some bit of it? Which bit?

The troops begin to work harder and harder, longer and longer hours. Despite this, something – either a project or some business as usual thing – starts to drift. Eventually, there's a bit of a stink about this thing. Some senior manager or customer begins to jump up and down about "their" thing. If they shout loud enough people are switched onto that thing and the thing that lost the people is told to work harder. They do – but it doesn't make any difference. *That* thing now starts to drift, despite the long hours being worked. And the thing to which people were moved doesn't necessarily speed up. There are learning curves and people need to come up to speed and they make mistakes that people who were already familiar with the thing had stopped making ages ago.

Life carries on like this until something else is seen to be drifting. The same events occur – a stink, jumping up and down, people being moved from one thing to another, the progress on more and more things not being what was expected.

Eventually, the end of the year comes round. Some things have been done, many haven't. Many have come in late and/or over-budget. Some people are burnt out and leave. Everybody thinks it was a tough year, but they worked really hard. There is a sense of having triumphed in the face of adversity. We sure earned our salaries and bonuses this year, we think. Yep – we did one hell of a job. And there's certainly no comparison between what we've done and the earlier car repair shop scenario. No comparison at all. Nossir, none.

Well, apart that is, from:

● Not having enough people to do all the work.

Oh, and:

● Not planning enough or properly.

And … well …there's:

● Constantly changing priorities and switching between jobs.

Not to forget:

● The wasted time, effort and money.

And, of course:

● Not knowing which jobs are going to be done and which jobs aren't.

No, apart from these, there are no comparisons at all.

Introduction

Look down the following list and see whether any of these things apply to your organisation:

- Priorities appear to be constantly changing.
- Everybody working long hours (10-16 hours a day) over sustained periods of time is standard practise.
- So-called 'fire fighting' is standard practise.
- There is no real culture of proper planning.
- Pressure and stress are so severe that they effect peoples' health.
- There is no sense of having a work/life balance. (Peoples' feelings about work may range from 'don't particularly enjoy working here' through to 'dread going to work in the morning').
- Projects are only completed with huge effort and overtime.
- Some projects are not completed at all or go badly astray.
- Nasty surprises are commonplace.
- There is a sense that there is a lot of wasted time, effort, resources or money. (This includes the same problem ending up being solved several times – or work having to be redone.)
- There is a feeling that while the way we do things at the moment may not be perfect, it's the best way there is. (And certainly anyone who questions the way things are done is probably met with some of the phrases below.)
- These things just described are believed to be 'part of the culture of the organisation'.
- There is a sort of permanent backlog which never seems to get cleared.
- Management use any of the following (or similar) phrases:
- "This is a very aggressive schedule/deadline";

- 'That's just the culture here'';
- "I don't want to hear anybody using the word 'can't''';
- "We like a can-do attitude here";
- "Don't bring me problems, bring me solutions";
- "You're going to have to learn to do more with less";
- "You're being inflexible";
- "You're not being a team player";
- "Work smarter, not harder";
- "Is this plan based on a five day week?";
- "You're lucky to have a job";
- "We don't have time to plan it, just go do it";
- "JFDI" [where the 'J' stands for 'just', the 'D' for 'do' and the 'I' for 'it'];
- "If you don't do it, I'll find somebody who will";
- "We have no choice – we have to do it";
- "That's not the kind of attitude we want around here";
- "We want can-do people here";
- "I don't think you're suited to the culture of this organisation".

If you've heard any one of these, then you'd better read this book.

For reasons that I'll explain in the next few chapters, organisations that have these characteristics end up being run with very large amounts of waste. This waste can come from up to seven different sources as described in Chapter 2. I refer to organisations that are run like this as "Big Waste" organisations.

Governments know and keep track of how many days are lost through sickness or strike action every year. Bizarrely, we haven't a clue – and we don't even try to measure – how many days are lost through badly run projects/initiatives/undertakings. One's sense though, is that the number must be colossal – dwarfing sick days, strike days and a whole lot more besides.

While the characteristics that I have described are commonplace, they are not inevitable or necessary. It is possible to run successful organisations where none of these things happen, where little or none of this waste occurs. For obvious reasons then, I call these organisations "Zero Waste" organisations.

This book covers everything you need to know to turn your

organisation into a Zero Waste one. Whether you are in the public or private sector, profit-making or not-for-profit, a company, a division, a department, a section, a team – whatever – you can take the ideas in this book and become an organisation where:

- Projects completing predictably on time and within budget are the norm. Projects going off the rails and nasty surprises are somewhat unusual.
- Your operation is the part of the organisation that works best.
- Priorities and changes of priority are clear to everybody and occur a lot less frequently than currently.
- In general, people work standard eight hour (or whatever is standard for you) days and late and weekend working is something of a rarity.
- There is a culture of proper planning. The maxim, 'a little planning is better than a lot of firefighting' is embedded in the organisation.
- You can know in five minutes if a project is in good shape or not.
- You can know right at the beginning of the year whether your targets are achievable or not.
- You can recognise the difference between 'stretch goals'/'aggressive schedules' and losing the plot.
- You get more done and spend less time doing it.
- You vastly reduce fire fighting and waste of time, effort, money and resources.
- You get projects done in the shortest possible time.
- You know how to respond correctly when you get handed an impossible mission.
- Pressure and stress are severely reduced.
- You still have a life.

The book is divided into three parts. Part 1 is called "The Basics" and has seven chapters. Chapter 1 describes how to know if you've got the condition that I've called Big Waste. It identifies the symptoms you will see in your organisation. You may have these symptoms but feel that you still don't have a Big Waste problem. Chapter 2 shows that you're probably wrong. It shows you where the waste is occurring. Chapter 3 offers a theory as to why Big Waste occurs. Chapter 4 summarises the steps that need to be taken to solve the problem of Big Waste and turn a Big Waste organisation into a Zero Waste one. Chapters 5, 6 and 7 describe some basic skills and knowledge that you and your organisation will need to make that journey.

Part 2 of the book, which has five chapters, explains how to install a Zero Waste system, i.e. it shows you the things you're going to have to do to begin the process of transforming your organisation.

Part 3 of the book has four chapters and describes how to move your organisation to Zero Waste.

In order to make the concepts as real as possible, I have used a made-up worked example. The example is of a medium-sized company (of about fifty people) in the technology products sector. Each chapter in Parts 2 and 3 shows how the ideas and concepts described would be applied in such an organisation. In addition, it will be made clear – if it isn't self-evident – how these ideas and concepts would be scaled up or down for bigger or smaller organisations.

Don't expect to find any complicated ideas in this book. The ideas are simple. But somewhere along the way it seems to me we have lost both the ability to look for simple solutions and the high regard in which such solutions should be held.

Anyway, the promise of this book is simple. Run a successful organisation and get home on time. If this appeals to you then turn the page and let's get started.

PART ONE
Chapter 1

Big Waste - How To Know
If You've Got It

Almost all organisations, no matter what sector or business they are in, operate in broadly the same way.

In a typical organisation this is what happens. At the beginning of the year, the owners or shareholders or board decide that they want to do "more" business as usual. They say they want to capture X per cent more customers or market share, increase revenue by Y or profit by Z, sell such and such a per cent more widgets and so on. They also want to do some brand new things – new products, services, initiatives, take new directions.

The management team takes this mission and launches a bunch of projects designed to make sure that both of these major thrusts (business as usual and new initiatives) are realised. They often say the kind of things mentioned in the Introduction. While some of these phrases may sound quite different from each other, they in fact all have common undertones. These undertones are:

- What we're being asked to do is really tough.
- But it's certainly doable.
- And we know you're the man/woman for the job.
- And if you say you can't do it, you're being disloyal in some way.
- And planning is for wimps – the way to get this done is just to go in and do it.

Everybody in the organisation now has (a) maybe a day job and (b) almost certainly, a project-related workload. Most management teams expect everybody to undertake this workload. For this reason planning becomes somewhat secondary. Indeed planning can come to be viewed as something of a problem. After all, we don't want plans showing us that the things we are trying to do are impossible, now do we?

Symptoms:

- There is no real culture of proper planning.
- Use of the phrases identical or similar to those in the Introduction.

Because plans are non-existent or inadequate, there is no real measure of whether there are enough people to do all the work. (You may have heard the old saying, "if you can't measure it, you can't manage it"). The suspicion (or it could be much stronger than that) is that that there aren't. But it doesn't matter – because somehow, the view is, we'll find a way. In reality, that "somehow" is generally pretty obvious and well known to everybody. If there aren't enough people to do all the work, then the existing people can just work harder. And this is exactly what happens – the troops begin to work harder and harder, longer and longer hours.

Symptom:

- Everybody working long hours (10-16 hours a day) over sustained periods of time is standard practise.

Despite this, something – either a project or some business as usual thing – starts to drift. (This is inevitable if there aren't enough people to do all the work.) Eventually – it's usually as late as possible because nobody wants to be seen to be the bearer of bad news – somebody realises that there's a problem.

Symptom:

- Nasty surprises are commonplace.

When this happens there's a bit of a stink. Some senior manager or customer begins to jump up and down about "their" thing. If they shout loud enough people are switched onto that thing and the thing that lost the people is told to work even harder.

Symptom:

- Priorities appear to be constantly changing.

They do work harder – but it doesn't make any difference. That or some other thing now starts to drift, despite the long hours being worked. And the thing to which people were moved doesn't necessarily speed up. There are learning curves and people need to come up to speed and they make mistakes that people who were already familiar with the thing had stopped making ages ago.

Life carries on like this until management realises that something else is drifting. The same events occur – a stink, jumping up and down, people being moved from one thing to another, the progress on more and more things not being what was expected. And so the year unfolds.

Symptom:

- So-called 'fire fighting' is standard practise.

Eventually the end of the year comes round. Some things have been done, many haven't. Many have come in late and/or over-budget. Right up to the last minute it's perhaps not been a 100% clear which things – out of all the things we set out to do at the beginning of the year – are going to end up being done and which are going to be left undone.

Symptoms:

- Projects are only completed with huge effort and overtime.
- Some projects are not completed at all or go badly astray.
- There is a sort of permanent backlog which never seems to get cleared.

- There is a sense that there is a lot of wasted time, effort, resources or money.

Some people are burnt out and leave. Everybody thinks it's been a tough year and that they worked really hard.

Symptoms:

- Pressure and stress are so severe that they effect peoples' health.
- There is no sense of having a work/life balance. (Peoples' feelings about work may range from 'don't particularly enjoy working here' through to 'dread going to work in the morning').

There is a sense of having triumphed in the face of adversity. We sure earned our salaries and bonuses this year, we think. Yep – we did one hell of a job.

Symptoms:

- There is a feeling that while the way we do things at the moment may not be perfect, it's the best way there is.
- These things just described are believed to be "part of the culture of the organisation".

If any of this sounded familiar, if you saw any of these symptoms in your organisation, then there's a fair chance that you've got Big Waste to a greater or a lesser extent.

But no, you're saying, you've got it all wrong. While we may have these symptoms, we don't have the problem. These are just the way we are, just normal characteristics of our organisation and the way we do business.

Really? Read on.

Chapter 2

Big Waste – Hey, That's Not Us!

"Whoa! Wait a minute", you say. "We may do and say some of the things you talk about, but we don't have a problem with waste"; or:

- "We're a start-up. We're lean and mean and hungry. There's not much flab in our organisation"; or
- "We've had to downsize. We're *having* to do more with less. You won't find much waste in *this* organisation"; or
- "We're in a very fast-changing sector. Priorities *do* change all the time"; or
- "This isn't a holiday camp. So what if we sweat our resources a bit"; or
- "Firefighting – it's the nature of our business"; or
- "All our competitors work this way. If we don't well that's the end of us"; or
- "We've got a great team here. They know what they're doing"; or
- "Not everyone is suited to working here".

All of this may or may not be true. But let me tell you the seven ways there may be waste in your organisation. If none of these apply to you, close the book and pass it along to somebody who needs it.

1. There is waste every time you switch people between projects.
Every time a so-called priority changes and you take people off one project/assignment and put them on to another, waste occurs. It occurs

on the project they come from because now that project has to reconfigure itself and see how they're going to get the thing done now. If they decide to just work longer hours to make the deadline then see #4 below. If they announce some kind of slip or delay then that's going to cause further downstream waste because what the project was meant to deliver (savings, revenues, profits) will now be delayed.

On the project they move on to, there will be waste as you bring them on board: bring them up to speed; they have a learning curve; they take time away from people already working on the project; you have to train them; they require hand-holding and nurturing. You have to find places for them to work, tools to work with and integrate them into the team. Don't forget too about Brooks' Law [2] – "adding people to a late project makes it later". So adding people to a project doesn't always speed it up; in fact, adding people to a project may have:

- Little effect
- No effect
- Could actually slow it down.

2. There is waste every time you don't plan a project properly

If you think about it, projects get done through a sequence of events. There are three ways this sequence of events can be built. Two of them are less efficient than the third. (I should also add that, in my experience, the third is the least widely used.)

The first way that you can build the sequence of events is not do anything at all – you just let fate or luck do it! Here's what working on such a project would be like. Charlie arrives in in the morning and says, "Hmmm, what'll I do today?" He does something. Then he realises he needs something from somebody else, so he wanders down the corridor and says, "Hey Fred, do you have that other thing?" But maybe Fred says he won't have that until Friday and so Charlie shrugs and does something else and so the project unfolds with things just ... well, sort of happening. Will there be waste on such a project? Is there bear poo in the woods?

Now clearly nobody would consciously do this and deliberately decide that they're going to let fate/luck run their project. But in your organisation today there are almost certainly projects that are being run exactly like this. Typically, they're not being run like this because people are stupid or incompetent. They're being run like this because people don't have *enough* time available to run the project. If people are too busy, are trying to keep too many balls in the air, are multi-tasking so much that they don't have time available to run the project, then fate/luck just takes over. But you need to remember that fate/luck is the worst project manager there is.

The second way you can build the sequence of events is to do it in real time. Here's what this is like. You arrive at work in the morning and look at your to-do list. You start doing the first thing on the list but then somebody asks you to come to the nine-thirty meeting. During the meeting, somebody knocks on the door and says, "Can I speak to you for a minute?" While you're speaking to them, your mobile phone rings so you answer that. Then your computer goes "bing!" because an email has arrived. And then your landline rings … You get the idea. You sort of ricochet through the day. Gotta go here, gotta go there, do that thing, talk to that guy … You may be familiar with the "f" word –"fire fighting".

Fire fighting is a term used to describe how you deal with crises or unexpected events. A fire fight occurs when something you didn't anticipate happens and you have to deal with it.

Now, absolutely fire fighting happens on projects. No matter how carefully they're planned, on your projects and my projects, fire fights are going to happen. But not everything that happens on a project is a fire fight. Many things that happen on projects could have been predicted – if only you'd thought about them. Fire fighting – the recipe for a short, unhappy life – is certainly not the way to run a project efficiently and without waste.

That leaves one other possibility when it comes to building the sequence of events. This is to do it right at the beginning – before you have made any commitments to any stakeholders, before you start hiring people or allocating jobs or burning up the budget – and build as much of the sequence of events as you can. Fire fights will still happen, but then you can save your energy for the things that are genuine fire fights; as opposed to the things which would never have become fire fights in the first place if only you had thought about them.

Building this sequence at the beginning has another name. It's called planning.

3. There is waste every time you have to deal with a fire fight

Whether you planned the project well or not, there is waste every time you have to deal with a fire fight. The more fire fights, the more waste. Over time you can reduce the amount of fire fighting you do by understanding why the fire fight occurred and factoring that into your planning next time around. But notice that that just leads you back to proper planning.

4. There is waste because people are working long hours

You may think that because people are working long hours over sustained periods you're sweating your resources and maximising your productivity. Think again, comrade.

Let's be clear. This is not about a short "push" to hit a deadline or make a milestone or solve a customer problem. This is about overtime (10-16 hour days) over long, sustained periods of time.

Burnout hours are bad because people quickly become less efficient than if they had just worked a normal forty hour week. While this may sound counter-intuitive, if you think about it you can see why this would be the case.

Imagine, first of all, that you were going to have the hottest date of your life at 8pm this evening. How would you organize your day? Well, to begin with, you'd probably plan to leave at, say, 5pm For you this would be a hard deadline every bit as vital as having to catch a plane, a train or pick up kids from the crèche. Just to be on the safe side, you might actually plan to have all your work done by 4pm. Then, if some genius did come in to you late in the day looking for something urgent, you would have an hour's contingency to deal with it.

You would plan your day carefully, figuring out exactly what had to get done so that you could leave by 4pm. You would be brisk with time wasters, not allowing them to take much of your time and in the process jeopardising your date. The result would be that the important things would get done and you would be ready by 4pm to go home, scrub up, put your glad rags on to get to your rendezvous.

Now contrast this with if you're coming in to face a day which will last from say 8am to 8pm or later. And this is not an isolated day. You have been doing this for a long time and, as far as you can tell, will continue to do it for the foreseeable future. Not only that, but you haven't been having weekends or evenings to recover from these days. And maybe you haven't been eating or sleeping very well. Or getting much or any exercise. And you haven't been seeing too much of your loved ones. In short, your life has narrowed to being at work, thinking about work, bringing work home with you, or cancelling other things so you can work.

Now, how will you spend your day? Well, you will be lazy with your time. Somebody wants to stop for a chat, you'll be happy to chat with them for ages. You may take long breaks or spend time messing around with your inbox or doing any number of other time-wasting things. This is because you know you have a vast amount of hours to spend each day and that if something doesn't get done today then there's always an equally vast number of hours tomorrow. In short – productivity goes out of the window.

So working burnout hours is bad in that it's just not productive. There is lots of attendance but not much achievement – at least not as much as there would be if you were going home on time. If you want a supporting opinion on this, read [1], especially Chapter 15.

5. There is waste every time a project goes astray or is cancelled.
In the former, there is waste because of the delayed benefits (savings, revenues, profit). In the latter there is the waste of all the time, energy, resources, effort and money that went into it.

6. There is waste because morale goes down
It's difficult to measure but this is the waste due to people's physical and mental health suffering. I both know of, and have heard numerous stories of, people who have suffered breakdowns through overwork on projects. Physical health suffers resulting in lost days through illness – never mind the effect on the people themselves.

And relationships suffer. With wives, husbands, partners, girlfriends, boyfriends, children, parents, siblings. I know of marriages that have broken up because of this issue. Or (especially) men wondering where their children's childhoods went. If their work is causing people to experience things like this, do you think that's going to be good for productivity?

7. There is waste due to multitasking

When people are multitasking, there is now additional work introduced. This is the put-down-pick-up overhead that occurs every time they have to lay one thing aside and pick up something else to work on it. As they put down, they (hopefully) try to organise the thing so that it'll be easy to pick up again. Then, as they pick it up, there is the work involved in getting their head around the new thing.

And here is a terrifying calculation.

Let's say that there's a job that has to be done on your project and you estimate it to be 10 man-days. Charlie's going to do it and Charlie's available full-time i.e. 5 days a week. Then the duration of this job is 2 weeks – 5 days the first week, 5 days the second week, job done.

Now supposing it was to happen that Charlie was only available one day a week and you know how easily this can occur. Charlie is involved in another project which was meant to have finished but it hasn't quite finished yet, so he has to spend time there. And Charlie is the only guy who knows about the X project or system or thing and there are some issues with that. And there's been a customer-related issue that Charlie's having to deal with ... You know how it goes.

With 1 day a week, Charlie's job will take 10 weeks. And this doesn't take into account that the job will now probably be bigger than 10 man-days now, because there is going to be the additional effect of Charlie putting it down and picking it up a week later. But never mind about that for now. This thing of "we-estimated-five-days-a-week-we-got-one" doesn't sound that serious. On a big project you mightn't even pick up that it had happened. On a small project, with Charlie sitting behind you, you mightn't pick up that it had happened. Yet, this one little thing, that doesn't appear that serious, can potentially cause a *two month* delay on this project (10 weeks minus 2 weeks).

And let's not forget the put-down-pick-up effect which now adds extra time to this job, making a bad situation worse. And remember that this is one job that belongs to one Charlie. Is this the only job of Charlie's that this is happening to? I don't think so. And is Charlie the only person to whom this is happening? Unlikely.

Another way to think about multitasking is with the idea of availability. The more multitasking a person does, the less availability they have to work on projects. Not knowing people's correct availability will just eat away at your project. You'll start and, almost immediately, you'll start to fall behind schedule. The team will work a bit harder, longer hours. But it won't do any good. You'll continue to slip. You'll be sending out status reports saying things like, "We've lost a bit of ground but we hope to make it up later in the project" – one of life's greatest illusions. One day you wake up and you're miles adrift of where you expected to be.

As I said earlier, if none of these seven apply to you, you can stop reading now.

Chapter 3

Why Big Waste Occurs

Why does Big Waste occur? Based on what I have seen during my own time in business, it seems to me that there are five reasons:

- Denial about the nature of supply and demand;
- Multitasking;
- Not understanding the significance of work/effort;
- We don't fight wars any more;
- Feeling that there's no better way.

Let's look at them in turn.

Denial about the nature of supply and demand
Do you ever think that you went into the wrong business? I do. I sometimes think I should have gone into the dieting/weight loss business. There's clearly plenty of money to be made there. Diets based on particular foods (the cabbage soup diet, for example), diets based on combinations or non-combinations of food groups (no proteins with carbohydrates or whatever), diets based on food with a particular property like the glycemic index (GI), the list goes on and on. And yet, as a society, we continue to get fatter. Good news for the dieting/weight loss business. There are going to be customers around for a long time to come.

I really want to write a diet book of my own. It's going to be called the *Supply and Demand Diet*. In fact, I have to confess – I've written it. Unfortunately though, I don't think I'm going to find a publisher for it.

You see, it's only got one page in it. And there aren't many words on the page. This is what it says:

'Losing weight is a problem in supply and demand. There is demand – the amount of calories you require each day. While it varies based on a number of factors, the average daily calorie requirement for women is about 2,000 calories while for men about 2,500. Then there is supply – the amount of calories you take in every day. If your supply exceeds your demand, you will put on weight. If your supply equals your demand, you won't lose weight. If your supply is less than your demand then you will lose weight.'

I mention all of this because being in denial about supply and demand is not a thing that is unique to business. It happens in other areas of life as well.

But it is business we are concerned with here and being in denial about supply and demand certainly happens. There is demand – the number of people we need to do a particular job or project – and there is supply, the people available to do that work. So let's say the job is estimated to last a week and require five people full-time. Then there are going to have to be five people full-time available to do the work or else the job won't get done in a week. If the people are only available half the time the job will take two weeks i.e. it will run late. But at least the job will get done. *But in order for jobs to get done supply must match demand.* You'll have heard the expression, 'it isn't black and white' and many things in life are like that – they don't have one definitive answer. Unfortunately, supply and demand *is* black and white. It *does* have one definitive answer and it's this – if there aren't people to do the work, the work won't get done.

Why am I banging on about such an obvious truth? Well, it's because, just as with weight loss, I have seen many people in denial about the simple fact of supply and demand. Let me give just one example.

Recently I was doing some training for a company and the course attendees were telling me about the management philosophy of their previous CEO. As they explained it, his approach was known as 'JFDI'. The 'J' stood for 'Just', the 'D' stood for 'Do' and the 'I' for 'It'. I'm assuming you can work out what the 'F' was for.

So the way this would work was – for example – there might be a meeting where his management team was explaining that they needed certain time, budget, resources to get a particular project done. There might be a certain amount of wrangling and negotiating but the CEO inevitably ended the meeting by standing up, gathering up his stuff, saying, "Look – JFDI!" and leaving the meeting. I should add that this is a publicly quoted company.

If this had been the first time I had come across this, it probably wouldn't have bothered me that much. I would have shrugged and said, "Glad I don't work there" and left it at that. But this attitude of JFDI is something that – in varying shades and flavours – I have come across in almost every company I have consulted to or trained in over the last twenty years. The notions of "JFDI", "we have no choice", "we have to do it", "that's not the kind of attitude we want around here", "you're being too inflexible", "if you don't do it, I'll find somebody who will", "you're lucky to have a job" – and worse – seem to have become standard operating procedure in many modern businesses, large and small. All of these organisations are in denial about supply and demand and this denial causes Big Waste to occur.

Multitasking

Next is the problem of so-called "multitasking" – working on more than one thing at the same time. Multitasking is interesting because it is both a symptom of Big Waste, i.e. evidence that it is occurring, and a cause in it own right.

Bosses/management like the idea of multitasking – keep the troops busy. But multitasking is a *terrible* idea. You saw in the last chapter the lengthening effect that can occur when somebody is multitasking as opposed to working full-time on just one thing. Let's look at this issue from a couple of other points of view.

Let's look first at productivity. Some of the work that we do in our lives is interrupt-driven type work. A quick question here, a phone call there, a one-line answer to an email dashed off. But much of the work that we have to do – and this is particularly true of projects – is work that requires large chunks of (ideally) uninterrupted time. If we can get that time the work will progress well and productivity will be high. Just to illustrate this, I'm writing this book at the moment. Now it turns out

I've managed to engineer it that I am doing no other things work-wise right now. I am free to concentrate on this book and nothing else. I am working full-time on it. As a result my productivity is soaring and I am routinely exceeding the daily word target that I am setting myself.

Similarly for you, if you can spend your five days a week on one and only one thing, your productivity will soar and you will make great progress. In reality, you will probably get the equivalent of four really solid days working on the project. The fifth will disappear in things like dealing with emails, meetings that you can't really wiggle out of, timesheets and other stuff that organisations tend to foist in people to a greater or a lesser extent. (I say "the equivalent of" because I'm not assuming that four days you spend are contiguous i.e. Monday, Tuesday, Wednesday, Thursday and the rest of the stuff on Friday. In reality it will be more fragmented than that, but you will still get those big blocks of time.)

Now what happens if you have to work on two things simultaneously? You probably get the equivalent of less than two good days on each of them – because of put-down-pick-up – and the fifth day goes as before. With three things to work on simultaneously, you probably get the equivalent of a good day on each, the fourth day goes on put-down-pick-up, the fifth day as before. With four things to work on simultaneously, you're now starting to get the equivalent of less than a day a week on each. In addition, the amount of put-down-pick-up time is now starting to become comparable to the time spent actually doing stuff. And your week has become very fragmented and you'll be starting to fall prey to the probably-no-point-in-starting-that-now syndrome.

With more than four things to work on simultaneously it's almost getting to the point where it's hard to see how anything actually gets progressed. In short, personal productivity nosedives. But organisational productivity also nosedives. Have a look at the following.

Imagine that there are three identical projects that have to be done. Each project is estimated individually to take nine months and is also sized at nine man-months work. Each project consists of the following phases and the phases have to happen in sequence:

Figure 3.1 Phases of project

Phase	Work (in man-months)	Duration (in months)
Requirements gathering	1	1
Design it	1	1
Build it	4	4
Test it	2	2
Give it to the customers	1	1
TOTAL	**9**	**9**

Each project requires 1 man-month worth of IT work during the Build phase. Some of the Build phase (2 man-months worth) has to be carried out, then the IT work has to be done, then the remainder of the Build Phase. The projects have to be done as soon as possible and it's now 1 January .

The typical solution to this is to do the following:

- Start the projects as soon as possible, i.e. on 2 January (1 January is a public holiday and nobody should be working!).
- Multitask the IT guy across the three projects. In other words he will do a third of a month on each project for three months. Being realistic, we'd better add in the put-down-pick-up time and let's estimate that to add an extra man-month to the three man-months.

So the plans for the three projects end up looking like Figure 3.2:

Figure 3.2 Three projects with multitasking

	Jan	Feb	Mar	Apr	May	Jun	Jul	Aug	Sep	Oct	Nov	De
Project A	R	D	B	B	B/IT	B/IT	B/IT	B/IT	B	T	T	G
Project B	R	D	B	B	B/IT	B/IT	B/IT	B/IT	B	T	T	G
Project C	R	D	B	B	B/IT	B/IT	B/IT	B/IT	B	T	T	G

The projects start on 2 January and finish on 31 December. (And remember this is with only one person across the three projects multitasking. In general, lots of people are multitasking. And in general there are lots of projects). In theory, during months May through August, the people (other than the IT guy) who are working on these projects are meant to be doing no work. In reality this is not what will happen. The IT guy will have questions and issues for them. And in addition, in all likelihood, they will spend some time on the projects anyway due to the effect of Parkinson's Law. ("Work expands so as to fill the time available for its completion").

Now, supposing instead we took a decision not to multitask the IT guy. Instead he would work full-time on one project to get it done; then move onto the next one and then the last one. Look at Figure 3.3 to see what that does to the three projects:

Figure 3.3 Three projects with no multitasking

	Jan	Feb	Mar	Apr	May	Jun	Jul	Aug	Sep	Oct	Nov	Dec
Project A	R	D	B	B	B/IT	B	T	T	L			
Project B	R	D	B	B		B/IT	B	T	T	L		
Project C	R	D	B	B			B/IT	B	T	T	L	

From the same 2 January start *they all finish earlier than they would have with multitasking.*

Not only that, an even better solution could be arrived at than that shown in figure 3.3. If we did what figure 3.3 suggests then most likely what would happen in May of Project B and May/June of Project C is some Parkinson's Law again – work would expand to fill the time available for its completion – the guy's would find things to do. They would slow down. They'd say, "we're waiting on the IT guy anyway – what's the rush?"

So to avoid this you could actually start projects B and C later, thus making these three extra man-months available for productive work. Figure 3.4 shows this.

Figure 3.4 Three projects with no multitasking and staggered starts

	Jan	Feb	Mar	Apr	May	Jun	Jul	Aug	Sep	Oct	Nov	Dec
Project A	R	D	B	B	B/IT	B	T	T	L			
Project B		R	D	B	B	B/IT	B	T	T	L		
Project C			R	D	B	B	B/IT	B	T	T	L	

In words – *two of the projects can start later and all three will finish earlier when there is no multitasking*. And remember, as always, this is with just three projects and *one* person multitasking.

Look at the waste involved in doing it with multitasking (Figure 3.2) and without (Figure 3.4):

- 3 man-months (1 on project A and 2 on project B) spent at the beginning of the year that could have been spent on other things.
- 1 man-month due to the IT guy's put-down-pick-up across the three projects (an estimate admittedly, but a reasonable one, I think).
- 6 man-months at the end of the year (3 on project A, 2 on project B and 1 on project C) when we could have been seeing the benefits of these projects.
- The waste due to Parkinson's Law.

Given that we're talking about a relatively tiny amount of project work here – a little over two man years (27 man-months) – I think you'll agree it's a colossal amount of waste. Multitasking causes *huge* waste in projects.

Not understanding the significance of work/effort

Around the mid-eighties the first PC-based project planning tools began to become available. This meant for the first time that such capabilities, which up until then had been the preserve of the large project management companies who could afford them, were now available to anyone who owned a PC. Before we knew it people would be coming to meetings with charts that looked like Figure 3.5.

Figure 3.5 'The plan'

ID	❶	Task Name	Duration	Start	Finish	Predece	2003 Nov Dec	Qtr 1, 2004 Jan Feb Mar	Qtr 2, 2004 Apr May
1		1 Finalize list of projects	3 days	Wed 05/11/03	Fri 07/11/03		Norman		
2		2 Establish Quality System Review Team	3 days	Wed 05/11/03	Fri 07/11/03		Michael		
3		**3 IMPROVEMENT**	**90 days**	**Mon 10/11/03**	**Fri 12/03/04**				
4		3.1 Gather problems with the process	60 days	Mon 10/11/03	Fri 30/01/04	1,2		QS Review Team	
5	✑	3.2 Improve the process as a result of 3.1	20 days	Mon 02/02/04	Fri 27/02/04	4		QS Review Tear	
6		3.3 Report (to EVERYONE) regularly	90 days	Mon 10/11/03	Fri 12/03/04	1,2		QS Review Te	
7		3.4 Release the new version (decide format)	10 days	Mon 01/03/04	Fri 12/03/04	5		Mark to resou	
8	▥	3.5 Put out proposed changes to client	20 days	Mon 02/02/04	Fri 27/02/04			Mark	
9		**4 COMPLIANCE & IMPROVEMENT**	**100 days**	**Mon 05/01/04**	**Fri 21/05/04**				
10	▥	4.1 Monitor implementation of the process	100 days	Mon 05/01/04	Fri 21/05/04				

Management would look at this Gantt Chart, the plan and approve it. But Gantt charts tell lies. At least, Gantt charts that look like this do. Because this chart, as I've presented it here and as they have been presented in millions of other situations, doesn't tell the full story. It shows *duration* (see Figure 3.5). It doesn't show work. And without work we don't have the full picture.

Figure 3.6 The plan shows work and not duration

ID	❶	Task Name	Duration	Start
1		1 Finalize list of projects	3 days	Wed 05/11/03
2		2 Establish Quality System Review Team	3 days	Wed 05/11/03
3		**3 IMPROVEMENT**	**90 days**	**Mon 10/11/03**
4		3.1 Gather problems with the process	60 days	Mon 10/11/03
5	✑	3.2 Improve the process as a result of 3.1	20 days	Mon 02/02/04
6		3.3 Report (to EVERYONE) regularly	90 days	Mon 10/11/03
7		3.4 Release the new version (decide format)	10 days	Mon 01/03/04
8	▥	3.5 Put out proposed changes to client	20 days	Mon 02/02/04
9		**4 COMPLIANCE & IMPROVEMENT**	**100 days**	**Mon 05/01/04**
10	▥	4.1 Monitor implementation of the process	100 days	Mon 05/01/04

Suppose for example, we have three projects as shown in Figure 3.7.

Figure 3.7 Plan with three projects

ID	O	Task Name	Duration	Start	Finish	Predecessors	Resource Names	Sep '10 23	30	06	Oct '10 13	20	27	04	11	18	25	Nov '10 01	08
1		Project #1	12 wks	Mon 30/08/10	Fri 19/11/10															
2		Project #2	6 wks	Mon 30/08/10	Fri 08/10/10															
3		Project #3	9 wks	Mon 20/09/10	Fri 19/11/10															

The three projects are estimated to require these amounts of work:

- Project #1 60 person-days;
- Project #2 40 person-days;
- Project #3 50 person-days.

A total of 150 person-days. And suppose, in addition, that there are 2 people available to work full-time on these three projects over the 12 week period. Then 12 weeks in 60 days (5 days a week) times 2 people is 120 person-days. Demand = 150 person-days, supply = 120 person-days. This dog isn't going to hunt! But management have already approved the plan and the team have already made the commitment.

When I explain on training courses (and as I will shortly here) the difference between work and duration, people sometimes ask,"why do you need to know the work?" The question is staggering. You need to know the work so that you can know how much stuff has to be done. Without it all you have is lines on a chart.

We don't fight wars any more

Had we been living a thousand years ago, there is a fair chance that – depending on what situation we were born into – a lot of us would have spent some or all of our time fighting. Even a hundred years ago, a good proportion of the population was involved in the armed services. And not just for show – they fought and died. Men and women did heroic things.

I don't know if you know the expression "a forlorn hope". A forlorn hope was a group of soldiers chosen to take the leading part in a military operation, such as an assault on a defended position, where the risk of casualties was high. It was likely that most members of the forlorn hope would be killed or wounded. A forlorn hope was typically led by a junior officer with hopes of personal advancement. You would have thought that there wouldn't have been much enthusiasm to be part of a forlorn hope. As it turns out, the opposite was often the case. If the officer leading the forlorn hope survived and performed courageously, he was almost guaranteed both a promotion and a long-term boost to his career prospects. As a result, despite the risks, there was often competition for the opportunity to lead the assault.

These days most of us don't get to do things like that – at least not on a battlefield. But we often get offered such opportunities in work. And just as in the, say, Peninsular War, the lure is the same – promotion and a long-term boost to career prospects. We carry on the way we do because:

- most of us like the idea of being a hero;
- all of us like the idea of promotion and a long-term boost to *our* career prospects;
- all of us like to be on the winning team;
- those of us who are senior enough like the idea of sending the troops off on a do-or-die mission.

Feeling that there's no better way

When I come across bosses like the JFDI one described previously, I am reminded of the First World War generals – dull, unimaginative, using the same old weary tactics to achieve limited results with immense suffering. Most businesses operate a "system" to get their work done, which revolves around pressure and aggressive targets. This system had evolved over many years. It is how they have always done things. And you know how it is with such systems. Niccolò Machiavelli, the Italian statesman put it well. He said, "It must be considered that there is nothing more difficult to carry out nor more doubtful of success nor more dangerous to handle that to initiate a new order of things."

So it is with these systems. They have evolved to the point where they're highly refined. They serve us well. Why should we change them? In short, pressure works. Why change it? And what's the alternative anyway? And the notion that there might be another solution, a solution based around blindingly simple ideas, is too outrageous to contemplate.

So in summary:

- Denial about the nature of supply and demand.
- Multitasking.
- Not understanding the significance of work/effort.
- We don't fight wars any more.
- Feeling that there's no better way.

Any solution that we come up with is going to have to take these things into account.

Chapter 4

The Solution to Big Waste

If you're of the school that believes that there's no better way to do all of this than the way you do it at the moment, then you're going to have to think again. I'm going to show you that there is. Our solution to Big Waste is going to be built on four main pillars:

- Knowing supply and demand.
- Reducing (or ideally, eliminating) multitasking.
- Proper planning of projects. This will include making sure that all plans are based on work, not just duration.
- Not thinking we need to be heroes by accepting impossible projects.

In doing this, I hope you can see that it tackles the five issues that I highlighted in the last chapter:

- Denial about the nature of supply and demand.
- Multitasking.
- Not understanding the significance of work/effort.
- We don't fight wars any more.
- Feeling that there's no better way.

The solution will be done in eight steps as follows;

1. Figure out where we are at the moment [Chapter 8]
It would be good to get a sense of what kind of shape you are in and how

big the problem is. So that's what you'll do first. You'll take a reading on how you're doing.

2. Measure the demand [Chapter 9]
As you might have expected, any attempt to solve the problem of big waste in your organisation must begin with supply and demand. You need to know what these are. So first you've got to measure the demand.

3. Measure the supply [Chapter 10]
Next, you've got to measure the supply.

4. Prioritise the projects [Chapter 11]
Given that you will almost certainly have more demand (work to be done) than supply (people to do the work), you now have to decide how you're going to choose what gets done and what doesn't.

5. Make the cut [Chapter 12]
And now the most painful bit. You actually choose what's going to get done and what isn't. You're probably going to find this the most difficult bit in practice. Remember though, that you can't shy away from this decision. If you don't decide what projects you want to get done then fate/luck will decide for you as described in Chapter 1. It's up to you.

When you've done these five things you will have a Zero Waste system in place, i.e. a system that's capable of getting you to Zero Waste. The next thing you have to do is to make that journey from where you are now. Doing this involves three elements.

6. Plan your projects [Chapter 14]
Make sure that all of your projects have proper plans. Once you get to this point you'll be able to measure how well your system is performing and compare the result against those of Step 1.

7. Track and report your projects [Chapter 15]
This is what you will do on an ongoing basis to keep your system running.

8. Get your projects done as quickly as possibly [Chapter 16]
This add-on will enable you to get your projects done in the shortest possible time.

You may be wondering what's involved in putting your Zero Waste in place. How long is it going to take and how much of your time is it going to chew up? To answer these questions I have included here a little plan or timetable of how something like this could unfold. The plan assumes two things:

- That you work 1 day per week on this. You will also need some time from some other members of your team.
- That your organisation is roughly of the size described in the worked example, i.e. about thirty or so projects.

While clearly the second assumption is going to vary from one place to the next, at least this will give you some feel for the time and effort involved. The plan in Figure 4.1 shows that in a month (4 weeks) you really could have your system in place.

Figure 4.1 Timetable for putting Zero Waste in place

Week 1:	Measure where you are.
Week 2:	Measure the demand.
Week 3:	Measure the supply.
Week 4:	Prioritise the projects and make the cut. System in place.

Before we can launch into any of this, however, there are a number of basic things that you have to be aware of. You may know a lot of these already, but whether you do or not they are summarised in the next three chapters. They concern respectively:

- How to estimate properly.
- How to run a successful project (for which you need to know how to estimate properly).

- How to say no to an impossible mission (for which you need to know how to run a successful project).

Chapter 5

How to Estimate Properly

If you think about it, running projects is the most difficult job in the world. This is because what we get asked to do is to make a prediction of the future (a plan) and then make that prediction come true. Given that none of us *can* predict the future and make that prediction come true, you can see how difficult running a project is.

When we do an estimate we take a shot at making a prediction. While we accept that our estimate won't be a 100% accurate, we have to equally accept the necessity for the estimate to be as accurate as possible. This means that our prediction must be as accurate as possible, i.e. it will have the smallest possible error in it and thus the greatest chance of coming true.

Therefore you can see that estimating is a key skill – it may actually be *the* key skill – for anybody tasked with running any kinds of projects. In this chapter I'm going to put in one place everything you need to know to carry out good estimating.

We're going to go through the following things:

- Some useful approximations.
- The difference between duration and work.
- Calculating the budget.
- Assumptions.
- How to estimate (with an example).
- How to estimate peoples' availability.

Some Useful Approximations

When you're estimating you'll find the following to be of use to you. They're approximations but they make the arithmetic easy and they're close enough for government work(!), as the saying goes. Can I also say at this point that I use the prefixes 'man-' and 'person-' interchangeably with no intention to offend anybody.

- Never mind that your contract says you have to work 37.5, or whatever it is, hours per week. For most estimating purposes, 8 hours = 1 day or 8 man-hours (MH) = 1 man-day (MD).
- 5 days in a week, 5 person-days (PD) = 1 person-week (PW).
- 20 days in a month, 20 person-days (PD) = 1 person-month (PM).
- 12 months in a year, 12 person-months (PM) = 1 person-year (PY).
- And, finally, while holiday entitlements and number of public holidays varies from country to country, 240 man-days (MD) = 1 man-year (MY) is good enough for most situations.

Duration And Work

There are two quantities known as 'duration' and 'work' and they are different. Pay close attention. This is very important.

Duration, sometimes also called elapsed time, is *how long* something is going to take. It is measured in the normal units of time – hours, days, months, and so on. The usual duration of a soccer match, for example, is 90 minutes. Durations are important because they enable you to figure out how long a particular job, or an entire project, is going to take. If you estimate the durations of all of the individual jobs in a project, then figure out which jobs depend on which other jobs, you can figure out the duration of the project.

But if you want to know how big a project is, or how many people you're going to need to get it done, or what it's going to cost, then duration isn't going to help you.

For that you need something called work (sometimes also called 'effort'). This is simply how much stuff has to be done. Work is measured in units like man-days, person-hours, person-years and so on. The work in a soccer match, for example, if you count two teams of 11 (22), a referee, two linesmen and a fourth official is 26 times 90 minutes, i.e.

2,340 person-minutes which (divide by 60) gives 39 person-hours.

Sometimes there is a link between duration and work – as there was in the soccer match example – and sometimes there's no link. An example of there being no link is when we, say, give somebody a document to review and give them a week to do it. There might be a man-hour's work in doing the review, but the duration is a week.

Finally, notice how work (and not duration) can enable you to work out the budget. If you know somebody's hourly or daily rate i.e. the price per man-hour or man-day, then you can figure out what a particular job is going to cost. Let's look at a little more at budgets.

Calculating the Budget

Here's all you need to know. Each job in your plan will have a cost associated with it. This cost can come about in one of three ways:

- Labour only – The cost of this job is the work (in say, man-hours or man-days) multiplied by the hourly or daily rate, as appropriate. Where can you get this hourly or daily rate from? Go ask the Finance people. If they can't give it to you, make some kind of assumption. A common assumption would be to say that the daily rate should be 2-3 times daily salary. (There is more about assumptions in a little while.)
- Labour plus other costs – The cost of this job is the labour cost (as just described) plus other costs – things like, travel, hotels, equipment, software, consumables, raw materials and so on. How can you estimate these? Three possibilities – ask a supplier, look on the Internet, or make an assumption.
- Subcontract – You are going to pay some supplier or subcontractor a fee to get this job done. In general, in this situation, you don't care how much work the supplier puts into it – since they are getting their fee. What you *do* care about though is how long the job is going to take, i.e. its duration and when it will actually be done.

Adding the budget for each individual job gives you the budget for the entire project. Easy as that.

Assumptions

As mentioned previously, the big problem in project management is that you have to predict the future. Another way to think about this problem is that you never have enough knowledge about the project. Or to be more precise, the only day you have complete knowledge about the project is the day that it ends – and then this knowledge is of no use to you in getting the project done. (It's a hell of a lot of use in terms of improving your estimating – of which more later.)

Assumptions are useful things – are very powerful things – because you make up knowledge. You pretend to know things that you don't. Here's an example. Let's say your project has some kind of testing phase in it. I'm not necessarily talking about technology projects here. Most projects have a part in them where you test that what you've done is good. Ask somebody to estimate this part of their project and they'll probably say something like, "How long is a piece of string?" or "It'll take as long as it takes". Their rationale is that since they don't know how many errors they're going to find when they come to test it, it's impossible for them to say anything other than "It'll take as long as it takes".

But with assumptions you can do much better than this. You can assume that you'll find 20, 50 or 1,000 errors, or that 10% of things tested will have errors in them, or 9.714%. You can assume whatever you like. If these assumptions can be based on what happened on previous projects, so much the better. Otherwise you just make up something that sounds reasonable. It's no more complicated than that. But then see what this gets you:

1. First testing run (assume 10% errors).
2. Fix these errors.
3. Second testing run (assume 5% errors).
4. Fix these errors.
5. Third and final testing run (assume no errors).

The assumptions enable you to add detail to your plan, which is a good thing.

There will come a time when you have to explain to the project's stakeholders what things are definite (i.e. knowledge) and what things are assumptions. But this is not that time. For now you can treat knowledge and assumptions the same. So, if you come to estimate a piece of your project, and you say, "I haven't a clue. I have no idea. We haven't decided this, we haven't decided that, so I have no way of knowing" – just make some assumptions and you will be able to estimate this piece of your project in great detail.

How to do good estimating
Here's the method for good estimating.

1. Get the people who are going to do the project to do the estimating. If that can't be done because maybe they haven't all been hired or assigned or identified, then use the people who have. If you don't know who's going to do the project, get somebody to help you. Maybe a colleague can help you when you estimate and you can help them when they estimate. If there are people who have done such projects before, see if you can tap into their knowledge. If there are specialist parts of the project (IT, for example) involve the people who have the specialist knowledge. The worst thing you can do is to do all the estimating by yourself. The more heads you have working on the problem, the smaller the error there will be in the estimates.

2. Identify the big pieces of work that have to be done to get the project done – sometimes called "phases". You don't have to be too accurate here. You're just trying to break a bigger problem down into smaller problems. You maybe don't know much about astrophysics, for example, but you can probably come up – pretty quickly – with the big pieces of work that have to be done to put a space probe on Venus. They're something like this:

- Put the space probe in a rocket.
- Shoot the rocket up in the air.
- Send it to Venus.
- Put it in an orbit around Venus.
- Take the space probe out.
- Put it down gently on the planet.
- Press 'Start'!

3. Notice that the big pieces of work give you natural 'milestones'. Milestones in project management are markers that you can put into your plan to give you a sense of what kind of progress you are making. The end of each of these big pieces of work could be treated a milestone.

4. Within each of these big pieces of work, identify the detailed jobs that have to be done. And if you're wondering how detailed is "detailed" then – this'll work for the vast majority of cases – you need to break everything down such that each job you identify is between 1-5 days duration or 1-5 person-days of work.

5. For each detailed job, be as specific and concrete as possible, i.e. rather than saying "requirements gathering" say "Charlie meets with the IT people for 2 days to explain his requirements". Using simple language to describe jobs is a good way to ensure this. Write the list of jobs so that a child could understand it. Avoid jargon, buzzwords and techno babble. Don't say something in a posh or complicated way if you can find a simple way to say it.

6. Use cause and effect. This is just a fancy way of saying that jobs don't exist in isolation and that each job triggers other jobs. So there are really two questions to ask. The first one is "what happens first?" Then, having written that job down, keep asking, "what happens next?" or "who does what?" until you've built your list (sequence) of jobs.

7. Where you don't know something, make an assumption.

8. List all the jobs in a structure which shows the project as being made up of the big pieces of work (phases), which in turn are made up of the smaller pieces. This is what is known in project management jargon as a Work Breakdown Structure or WBS.

9. Lay all this information out in a Gantt Chart. (The example which follows illustrates a Gantt Chart).

Example
Here's what this method looks like when it's used on a real project. Let's

take what could be a real project and let me show you enough of this working so you get the gist of it.

Let's say that the project is to change some business process that we currently have. So right now, we do things a certain way, but now we're going to change that to a new way of working. The change will involve not just changes to what people do but also to the computer system that they use. Let's use our method to build a piece of the plan for this project. And let's do it a step at a time.

Example – Step 1 Jobs

More than one person to do the estimating? Yes – we have you and I.

The big pieces of work. OK, how about this:

1.   Figure out what changes have to be made (to processes, to the computer system).
2.   Make the changes to the processes.
3.   Make the changes to the computer system.
4.   Document the new way of working.
5.   Train everybody in the new way of working.
6.   Test that everything works.
7.   Go live.

Now let's take one of these big pieces and break it down into the detailed jobs. Let's take '6. Test that everything works' on the basis that it's furthest away in time and, so, the most difficult to know anything about.

'6. Test that everything works' can begin when big pieces 1-5 have been done. So let's use our method. What happens first? We have to figure out what we're going to test. And what happens next? We get some people to carry out the tests. And what happens next? They find errors. And what happens next? We fix the errors. And what happens next? They test again and find more errors.

You see how it goes. So here's what this might look like when we write it all down.

6.   Test that everything works:
6.1. Figure out what we're going to test.

6.2. Set up a test environment.

6.3. Get some people to carry out the tests and report errors.

6.4. Fix the errors.

6.5. Repeat 6.3 and 6.4 a number of times.

OK, so the next question is what does "a number of times" actually mean? Well, clearly we don't know how many reiterations of finding and fixing errors we're going to have to do. So what do we do? Hey, we make an assumption. And just for simplicity here and to keep the example manageable, let's assume three times. So:

6.   Test that everything works:

6.1. Figure out what we're going to test.

6.2. Set up a test environment.

6.3. Get some people to carry out the tests and report errors.

6.4. Fix the errors.

6.5. Repeat 6.3 and 6.4 three times.

Example – Step 2: Work

Now let's estimate the work in each of these jobs.

6.1. Figure out what we're going to test. This involves somebody writing some kind of test plan. Let's assume that one person can do this in five days. That's 5PD (person-days).

6.2. Set up a test environment. Let's assume that 1 person can do this in 3 days. 3PD.

6.3. Carry out the tests and report errors. Let's assume that 3 people are required to carry out the tests and it takes them 2 days each. That's 6PD. Let's write that like this (Figure 5.1):

Figure 5.1 Step 2: Work – 6.3 (Round 1)

	Testing	Fixing
First test round	6	

6.4.   Fix the errors. Let's assume that we find 10 errors. Let's further assume that out of these 10, 1 is Big, 3 are Medium and the other 6 are Small. And finally, let's assume that it takes 3 days to fix a Big error, a day to fix a Medium and that a Small can be done in half a day. (Please be clear that I'm just making these numbers up. If they can be based on previous experience that's great, but otherwise you just make the best guess you can.) So then the total work involved in fixing the errors is 1 x 3 + 3 x 1 + 6 x 1/2 = 9 PD.

For the second test round let's assume that we test everything again, not just the things that were wrong the first time and got fixed. (This is because we want to ensure that by fixing the things we fixed, we didn't introduce errors into things that worked right the first time.) So it's a second 6 PD. Let's assume that the second time out we get a smaller number of errors – say, no Big, 1 Medium, 4 Small. This gives 3 PD (1 x 1 + 4 x 1/2).

Finally, in the third test round, our three testers do 1 day of testing each and we assume that everything works perfectly and that there is no further fixing required (see Figure 5.2).

Figure 5.2 Step 2 Work – 6.3 (Round 3)

	Testing	Fixing	Altogether
First test round	6	9	15
Second test round	6	3	9
Third test round	3	0	3
Totals	**15**	**12**	**27**

So now all our estimates can be written as in Figure 5.3:

Figure 5.3 – Step 2: Work (Summary)

	JobWork (in person days)
6 Test that everything works	
6.1 Figure out what we're going to test	5
6.2 Set up a test environment	3
6.3 Carry out the tests and report errors (first round)	6
6.4 Fix the errors (first round)	9
6.5 Carry out the tests and report errors (second round)	6
6.6 Fix the errors (second round)	3
6.7 Carry out the tests and report errors (third round)	3
Total	**35**

Example – Step 3: Dependencies and Duration

To show the durations we're going to need a calendar, so let's show the work we've done so far but this time on a Gantt Chart. Here it is as Figure 5.4:

Figure 5.4 Step 3 – Gantt Chart showing work

Jobs	Work (person days)
START	0
1 Figure out what changes have to be made	
2 Make the changes to the processes	
3 Make the changes to the computer system	
4 Document the new way of working	
5 Train everybody in the new way of working	
6 Test that everything works	35
6.1 Figure out what we're going to test	5
6.2 Set up a test environment	3
6.3 Carry out the tests and report errors (first round)	6
6.4 Fix the errors (first round)	9
6.5 Carry out the tests and report errors (second round)	6
6.6 Fix the errors (second round)	3
6.7 Carry out the tests and report errors (third round)	3
7 Go live	
END	

Then let's add the dependencies – what depends on what, as in Figure 5.5:

Figure 5.5 Step 3 – Gantt Chart showing work and dependencies

Depends on	Jobs	Work (person days)
-	**START**	**0**
	1 Figure out what changes have to be made	
1	**2 Make the changes to the processes**	
2	**3 Make the changes to the computer system**	
2,3	**4 Document the new way of working**	
4	**5 Train everybody in the new way of working**	
5	**6 Test that everything works**	**35**
	6.1 Figure out what we're going to test	5
6.1	6.2 Set up a test environment	3
6.2	6.3 Carry out the tests and report errors (first round)	6
6.3	6.4 Fix the errors (first round)	9
6.4	6.5 Carry out the tests and report errors (second round)	6
6.5	6.6 Fix the errors (second round)	3
6.6	6.7 Carry out the tests and report errors (third round)	3
6	**7 Go live**	
7	**END**	

Now let's figure out the durations for the jobs in '6. Test that everything works'.

6.1. *Figure out what we're going to test.* We said that this was one person for five days. Thus the duration is 5 days.
6.2. *Set up a test environment.* We said that 1 person can do this in 3 days. 3 days duration.
6.3. *Carry out the tests and report errors (round 1).* We said 3 people for 2 days. Thus, the duration is 2 days.
6.4. *Fix the errors (round 1).* We haven't said how many people are fixing the errors, so let's make an assumption about that now. Let's assume we have three people to fix errors and that any one of them can fix any particular error. (In reality, this is probably an oversimplification, but let's not complicate this example unduly.) Thus, 9PD's worth of work will take 3 people 3 days.
6.5. *Carry out the tests and report errors (round 2).* This is 2 days again.

6.7. *Fix the errors (round 2).* 3PD's work to do, 3 people, that's 1 day's duration.

6.8. *Carry out the tests and report errors (round 3).* We said this would be 1 day.

So now let's add the calendar to our Gantt Chart (see Figure 5.6):

Figure 5.6 Step 3 – Gantt Chart showing work, dependencies and durations

Depends on	Jobs	Work (person days)	Duration (days)
-	START	0	
	1 Figure out what changes have to be made		
1	2 Make the changes to the processes		
2	3 Make the changes to the computer system		
2,3	4 Document the new way of working		
4	5 Train everybody in the new way of working		
5	6 Test that everything works	35	
	6.1 Figure out what we're going to test	5	5
6.1	6.2 Set up a test environment	3	3
6.2	6.3 Carry out the tests and report errors (first round)	6	2
6.3	6.4 Fix the errors (first round)	9	3
6.4	6.5 Carry out the tests and report errors (second round)	6	2
6.5	6.6 Fix the errors (second round)	3	1
6.6	6.7 Carry out the tests and report errors (third round)	3	1
6	7 Go live		
7	END		

Example – Step 4 Budget
And finally, let's do the budget for the jobs in '6. Test that everything works'.

6.1. *Figure out what we're going to test.* We said that this was 5PD. Let's assume there are no other costs and that Finance gives us a figure of 400 euros a day as the average daily rate.

6.2. *Set up a test environment.* We said that 1 person can do this in 3 days, so that's 3PD at 400 euros per day. Let's assume that we also have to buy some additional software to set up that test environment and we find out – by checking with our local software supplier – that this costs 1,500 euros.

6.3. *Carry out the tests and report errors (round 1).* Let's assume we don't have enough people to do the testing and so we subcontract this to a company that does testing. (I'm not saying that this is particularly realistic but it just enables me to show all three types of budget elements in our example.) Let's say they charge us a fee of 7,500 euros.

6.4. *Fix the errors (round 1).* 9PD's worth of work at 400 euros per day.

6.5. *Carry out the tests and report errors (round 2).* This is included in the 7,500 euros fee.

6.6. *Fix the errors (round 2).* 3PD's work to do at 400 euros per day.

6.7. *Carry out the tests and report errors (round 3).* This is included in the 7,500 euros fee.

So here's our Gantt Chart with the budget shown (see Figure 5.7):

Figure 5.7 Step 4 – Gantt Chart showing work, dependencies, durations and budget

Depends on	Jobs	Work (person days)	Duration (days)	Budget €	1 2 3 4 5 6 7 8 9 10
-	START	0			
	1 Figure out what changes have to be made				
1	2 Make the changes to the processes				
2	3 Make the changes to the computer system				
2,3	4 Document the new way of working				
4	5 Train everybody in the new way of working				
5	6 Test that everything works	35		17,000	
	6.1 Figure out what we're going to test	5	5	2,000	
6.1	6.2 Set up a test environment	3	3	2,700	
6.2	6.3 Carry out the tests and report errors (first round)	6	2	7,500	
6.3	6.4 Fix the errors (first round)	9	3	3,600	
6.4	6.5 Carry out the tests and report errors (second round)	6	2	-	
6.5	6.6 Fix the errors (second round)	3	1	1,200	
6.6	6.7 Carry out the tests and report errors (third round)	3	1		
6	7 Go live				
7	END				

How to estimate availability

You don't just have to know how to estimate projects. You'll remember what we said about the negative effects of multitasking. If you're to begin to manage these effects – another case of if you can't measure it, you can't manage it – then you're also going to have to be able to measure how much people are multitasking. Or to put this another way, you're going to have to measure their availability.

Supply-Demand Calculator

The Supply-Demand Calculator is the fancy name for something that we also call a "Dance Card". The name "Dance Card" refers to those more genteel times where, when women went to dances or balls, they were given a card with a list of the tunes that the band or orchestra was going to play. To dance with a woman a gentleman wrote his name against a particular dance, i.e. he booked that dance with that woman. The Dance Card measured supply (the number of dances available) and demand (the number of dances booked).

To calculate your Dance Card, your supply and demand, do the following.

Figure out everything you have to do – Demand

1. Pick a period of time – a month, a couple of months, from now to the end of next month, from now to the end of the quarter, half a year, the rest of the year – whatever suits you.
2. Make a list of all the projects you will be working on during the period that you've chosen. Include on the list any project which:

*   Ends during the period that you've chosen.
*   Starts during the period you've chosen.
*   Starts and ends in the period you've chosen.
*   Runs through the period that you've chosen.

Now add to the list what might be called "business as usual" or "day-job" type things. These would be things like:

*   *Meetings*. All your meetings may be about particular projects, but most of us have things like "the group meeting", "the Monday meeting", "company meeting" and so on. Don't forget too that you may have to do preparation before a meeting, there will be the meeting itself and you may have to do follow-ups or action items afterwards.
*   *Reports*. Maybe your job involves producing (or reading) a lot of these.
*   *Interruptions*. Whether they come person-to-person or by phone (landline or mobile), every one of us has these every day.
*   *Inbox/Email*. Possibly all of your emails are related to specific projects, but most of us have other stuff we have to deal with

every day. And anyway, there's the time involved in figuring out whether they're about specific projects or not.

- *Trips/Visits.* Maybe you're going on a business-related trip or somebody's coming to visit you and that will soak up your time.
- *Training.* Maybe you're involved in some form of training course or you're coaching or mentoring somebody else.
- *Annual leave/vacation/holidays.*
- *Managing people.* Maybe you're the line manager of a number of people and this takes up your time.
- *Phone calls/conference calls.* We all have some/a lot of these to do every day.
- *Support.* Maybe you support products or systems or people in some way.
- *Recruitment.* Maybe your organisation is expanding and you have to spend time looking at resumes, interviewing people and doing related activities.
- *Firefighting.*
- *Filling in for people.* Maybe you're standing in for people who are away on some kind of leave.

3.   Add an additional line item called, "New stuff". It may be that in your job nothing is going to change over the period that you're looking at. (I've heard there are jobs like that though I've never come across one myself!) Presumably, what's more likely is that new things will come along. We don't know what they are yet because they haven't come along – we just know it's inevitable that they will. "New stuff" is to cover these.

Figure out how much time it will take to do it

Now figure out how much of your time is going to go into each of the items on your list over the period that you're looking at. Use hours per day, days per week, total, hours, total days or whatever measure seems most appropriate to each line item. Be sure to record each of the amounts of time in the same units. I find days are best for this.

Add all of these up. This gives you the total amount of work you have to do in the period in question.

Figure out how much time you have available – Supply

Now figure out how many work days there are in the same period. (Convert that number to hours if you've been using hours in the previous section.) This is how much time you have available.

We have a little Excel spreadsheet called a Supply-Demand Calculator that will enable you to do this quickly. It's shown here as Figure 5.8. If you want a copy, send me an email at the address given on page 8 and I'll send it to you.

Figure 5.8 Supply – Demand Calculator

4/04/2011	ETP availability Calculator		
		Hours	**Days**
YOUR PROJECTS	**Project names**		
1		0	0	Number
2		0	0	Number
3		0	0	Total nun
4		0	0	Number
5		0	0	Total nun
6		0	0	
...		0	0	
BUSINESS AS USUAL / 'DAY JOB'			
Preparing / writing reports		0	0
Attending training		0	0
Training other people		0	0
Managing people		0	0
Annual Leave		0	0
Email / Inbox		0	0
Interruptions		0	0
Phone calls		0	0
Trips		0	0
Visits		0	0
Meetings		0	0
Filling in for people		0	0
Recruitment		0	0
Public holidays		0	0
Other		0	0
New stuff		0	0
	TOTAL	0	0

ETP Availability Calculator

Step	Cell(s)	Description	Action
1	L4	The number of weeks for which you want to calculate availability	Accept the default of 4 weeks or enter to override
2	L5	The number of days per week that you work	Accept the default of 5 days per week or enter to override
3	L6	Total number of work days in the period that you've chosen	Calculated (L4 multiplied by L5).
4	L7	The number of hours per day you work	Accept the default of 8 hours per day or enter to override
5	L8	The number of hours per week you work	Calculated (L6 multiplied by L7)
6	B4 - B10	The names of your projects. Include any project which starts, ends, starts and ends or passes through the period you've chosen	Enter the names of your projects
7	B13 - B26	Business as usual / 'Day job' things	Select which of these apply to you
8	B28	This is to cover new things that come along in the next 4 weeks. (In most jobs it's inevitable that new things will come along.)	No action
9	Columns C and D	Column C is your time measured in hours; column D your time measured in days.	Choose either hours (column C) or days (column D) as the units for recording your time. If you chose hours then carry out Steps 10-12. If you chose days then carry out Steps 13-15.
10	C4 - C10	The amount of your time (in hours) that will go into each of these projects over the next 4 weeks.	Estimate it in total hours or hours per day (and then multiply by the total number of days (L6))
11	C13 - C26	The amount of your time (in hours) that will go into each of these over the next 4 weeks.	Estimate it in total hours or hours per day (and then multiply by the total number of days (L6))
12	C28	The amount of your time (in hours) that will be soaked up by new things over the next 4 weeks.	Estimate / guess it i.e. pick a number
13	D4 - D10	The amount of your time (in days) that will go into each of these projects over the next 4 weeks.	Estimate it in total days or days per week (and multiply by 4)
14	D13 - D26	The amount of your time (in days) that will go into each of these over the next 4 weeks.	Estimate it in total days or days per week (and multiply by 4)
15	D28	The amount of your time (in days) that will be soaked up by new things over the next 4 weeks.	Estimate / guess it i.e. pick a number
16	C30	Total work you have to do in the next 4 weeks (in hours)	Calculated
17	D30	Total work you have to do in the next 4 weeks (in days)	Calculated
			Now you can compare C30 with L8 or D30 with L6 to see how much time is available

Examples

Here are a couple of examples of supply demand calculations just to help you in drawing up your own. Figure 5.9 contains one for a six month period. (The calculations assume 20 days in a month and 4 weeks in a month.)

Figure 5.9 Supply demand calculation #1

Job	120 Needs	20 Jan	20 Feb	20 Mar	20 Apr	20 May	20 Jun
Project X	72 days	12	12	12	12	12	12
Project Y	24 days	8	8	4	4		
Project Z	10 days				2	4	4
Selling	2 dpw	8	8	8	8	8	8
email/ Inbox/ Admin	1.25 dpw	5	5	5	5	5	5
Holidays	10 days						10
Total work to do	**194**	**33**	**33**	**29**	**31**	**29**	**39**

The column headed "Job" lists all of the things that this person is involved in. The next column indicates how much work is estimated to go into these things over the period under investigation. Days per month (dpm), days per week (dpw), hours per day or just plain days are all good ways of calculating how much work needs to be done. Then the remaining columns show how this time will be spread out over the period under investigation – in this case, six months.

There are two other items of interest. The top row shows how many days are available per month. The total of these is 120. (Note that rather than trying to allow for the different numbers of working days in different countries, I have assumed that every month consists of 20 days. You could adjust this up or down for your own situation. For example, in Europe, December is definitely not 20 working days in most companies.) The other item of interest is the total of all the work this person has to do – in this example, 194 days. In the example then, the person has an overload of more than 50%, i.e. over 50% more work to do than time available to do it.

The supply demand calculation in figure 5.9 was for a person who does a mixture of projects – which take reasonably predictable amounts of time – and other kinds of work. However, supply demand calculations can be done by anybody – even if your work is very unpredictable.

If your job is like that, then the best thing to do is to record what actually happens, say, in a particular week or over several weeks, and use this as your start point. Figure 5.10 shows a supply demand calculation for such a job, with actual time spent in a given week.

Figure 5.10 Supply demand calculation #2

#		Total hours	8 Mon	8 Tue	8 Wed	8 Thu	8 Fri	0 Sat	0 Sun	40
1	Phone calls	9.25	2.25	2.50	3.00	1.00	0.50	0.00	0.00	
2	Admin.	7.50	1.75	0.50	0.75	1.50	3.00	0.00	0.00	
3	Status report to boss	1.00					1.00			
4	Running office	4.75	1.00	0.50	1.00	1.00	1.25	0.00	0.00	
5	Overseeing staff	6.25	2.00	1.00	1.00	1.25	1.00	0.00	0.00	
6	E-mail, timesheets, petty cash, stock, phone	5.25	1.00	1.25	0.75	0.75	1.50	0.00	0.00	
7	Interruptions	7.50	1.00	0.50	2.50	2.00	1.50	0.00	0.00	
8	Meetings	6.25	0.00	0.75	1.50	3.00	1.00	0.00	0.00	
9	Bringing work home	6.00		3.00				0.00	3.00	
		53.75	9.00	10.00	10.50	10.50	10.75	0.00	3.00	

OVERLOAD 34%

Chapter 6

How to Run a Successful Project

Now that you know how to estimate properly, you're ready to take that knowledge and build around it a method or recipe for running any project successfully. Armed with this method, you'll also be in a position to assess any project very quickly. You'll be able to do this by looking at how closely or not the project you're assessing adheres to the recipe that you've learnt.

The project management approach is described in the rest of this chapter and is that described in my book, *How to Run Successful Projects III* [3]. This method has three key characteristics:

- It works. It has been used on some pretty significant projects. (It was used by the team who planned the Special Olympics World Games, the world's biggest sporting event in 2003.) Nobody has ever phoned me up and said, "I did it and it didn't work".
- It's common sense – simple to learn and easy to use.
- It's "light", i.e. it gets the project done with the least amount of effort on the part of the project manager.

Overview of the project management method
The method has ten steps in it. Five of these steps are to do with building a plan for the project and the other five are to do with executing the plan.

Not all of the steps are equally important and so there is a weighting attached to each of the steps. The weightings add up to 100 and, at any time over the life of your project, you can score your project out of 100.

This score is called a Probability of Success Indicator or PSI. The PSI tells you how likely or not your project is to succeed. Think of it as checking for the project's "vital signs", just as an A&E doctor does. Low weightings point you at the weak areas in your project, i.e. those that you must fix if your project is to succeed. The steps and weightings are listed in Figure 6.1 as follows:

Figure 6.1 Weighting of Steps in Project Management

Weighting	Step
PLANNING THE PROJECT	
20	1. Figure out the goal of the project
20	2. Make a list of jobs
10	3. The project must have one leader
10	4. Find people to do the work
10	5. (a) Put a margin for error in the plan; (b) Manage peoples' expectations
EXECUTING THE PLAN	
10	6. Use an appropriate leadership style
10	7. Know what's going on
10	8. Tell people what's going on
0	9. Repeat steps 1 through 8 until the project is over
0	10. Do a post mortem or review on the project

The steps are discussed in turn. The essentials of each step are given under the heading "The idea". Then there is a section called "What to do" on how to apply that step. Finally, the step is illustrated by an example.

Step 1 Figure out the goal of the project

1.1 The idea

The biggest single reason why projects go wrong is that they were never possible in the first place. It is important to realise that when a project is given to you, you are also – almost invariably – given what we might call constraints. Constraints can come as:

- Time – the project must be done by a certain date.
- Money – the project must be done for a certain budget.
- Resources – the project must be done with a certain group of people.
- Scope – what the project has to deliver has already been decided;
- Or some combination of the above.

If you try to both plan the project realistically *and* deal with the constraints at the same time, you will potentially get yourself into a lot of trouble. Therefore we do these two things separately. First we build a plan as if there were no constraints (using steps 1-4 & 5(a) and then we deal with the constraints in step 5(b)).

To fix the goal of your project, you need to take account of three things:

- You must establish a boundary around your project and say: "These things within the boundary are part of my project and these things outside are not" ("in scope" and "out of scope").
- Changes to the boundary will occur over the life of the project. When a change occurs on a project you have only three possible ways of dealing with it:

  – It's a big change. Changes to the agreed project scope, changes to the agreed project resourcing or assumptions turning out not to be true all constitute big changes.
  – Use contingency.
  – Work more hours.

- You must pick the right boundary i.e. the one that keeps all of the stakeholders in the project as happy as possible. (A "stakeholder" is any person or organization affected by the project.)

1.2 What to do

1. Identify the constraints and put them to one side for the moment.
2. Answer the question "how will I know when this project is over?"/"What point in time marks the end of this project?"/"What is the final event that marks its conclusion?" This will tell you the goal of the project.
3. Make a list of all the stakeholders. For each stakeholder, write down their "win conditions", i.e. write down what they would regard as a successful project. (Find out by asking them.)
4. When you've done this, go to step 2.

1.3 Example

Your boss comes into you and asks you to "run a job advertisement" for a particular kind of person. She says it needs to be done by the end of the month.

The constraint is the end of the month deadline. When is this project over? Not the trivial question it might first appear. Often project goals are phrased very loosely. Is this project over when the advert runs in the paper, or when you get CVs in response to the ad, or when you interview some people, or when you hire somebody, or what? All these are potentially valid endings to this project. You clarify this with your boss. Say it turns out to be just running the ad.

Stakeholders and their win conditions? Here they are displayed in Figure 6.2 overleaf.

Figure 6.2 Stakeholders and their Win conditions

Stakeholder Win conditions	
Us	Run ad that reflects well on the company and doesn't upset anybody. It also should communicate why the jobs on offer are so attractive that you'd be mad not to apply.
Our boss	The ad sends out a positive message about the company
Existing employees	Doesn't upset anybody – uses only material that is in the public domain
Potential employees	Sends out a message that the company is one that people want to work for
Our customers	Sends out a message that the company is expanding, and is a good company to do business with.

Step 2 Make a list of jobs

2.1 The idea
This is where you do the estimating as described in the previous chapter.

2.2 What to do
Look back on the previous chapter if you're in any doubt. Then go to step 3.

2.3 Example
Here's a possible piece of Work Breakdown Structure related to the user testing of an IT system (see Figure 6.3).

Figure 6.3 Work Breakdown Structure

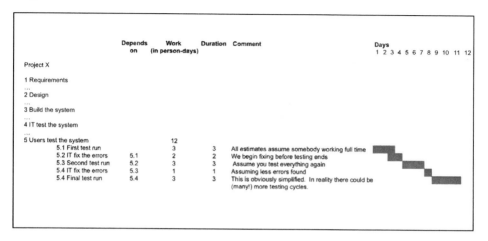

Step 3: The project must have one leader

3.1 The idea

Your project must have one leader, one person who ensures that all the jobs identified in the previous step get done. Project Manager is not just a title. It is a real job with real duties, and those duties involve doing whatever has to be done, to ensure that all of the jobs identified in step 2 are completed. Obviously, these duties can only be carried out if you set time aside to do them. A good rule of thumb is to take 10% of the total effort (not duration) in your project, and add this on for project management.

3.2 What to do

1. Calculate 10% of the total effort (not duration) in your project.
2. Put an additional job in your Work Breakdown Structure called 'Project Management', with the amount of effort from 1. above.
3. Go to step 4.

3.3 Example

*   There are four people working full-time on your project for 10 weeks.

- Total effort = 4 people x 10 weeks = 40 person-weeks = 200 person-days
- 10% of this = 20 person-days
- Spread out over 10 weeks, this means that this project will require – on average – 2 days project management per week.

Step 4 Find people to do the work

4.1 The idea
Like many things in life, project management is a problem in supply and demand. The demand comes from the work to be done (identified in step 2); the supply comes here, in this step. Essentially, if there are 100 person-days worth of work to be done, there are going to have to be 100 person-days worth of people to do the work.

The problem arises, of course, because the demand (work to be done) has a tendency to go up ("Can we just have this one extra thing?", "I thought that was already included", etc) and the supply has a tendency to go down and down and down ("There are no resources available", "We need Charly for this other project", "Sorry, I'm not going to be able to do that for another week" etc).

Your job here is to ensure that there are people to do all the jobs and that those people have time available to carry out the jobs.

4.2 What to do

1. Put peoples' names against all the jobs in your Work Breakdown Structure.
2. Find out how much each person is available to do each job. If a job is 10 person-days and Charly is available 1 day per week, the job will last 10 weeks; if she's available full-time it will last only 2 weeks – a huge difference.
3. Store all of the resulting information in a Gantt Chart – a chart showing who does what when. A sample piece of Gantt chart is given in the example. It continues the example from section 2.3, see Figure 6.4 below.
4. Go to step 5(a).

4.3 Example

Figure 6.4 Extended Gantt Chart

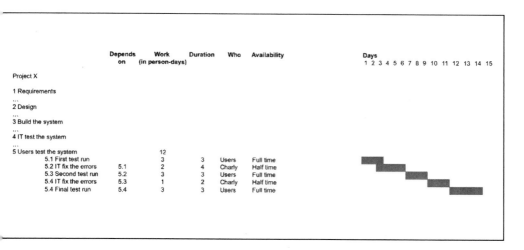

	Depends on	Work (in person-days)	Duration	Who	Availability		Days 1 2 3 4 5 6 7 8 9 10 11 12 13 14 15
Project X							
1 Requirements							
...							
2 Design							
...							
3 Build the system							
...							
4 IT test the system							
...							
5 Users test the system		12					
5.1 First test run		3	3	Users	Full time		
5.2 IT fix the errors	5.1	2	4	Charly	Half time		
5.3 Second test run	5.2	3	3	Users	Full time		
5.4 IT fix the errors	5.3	1	2	Charly	Half time		
5.4 Final test run	5.4	3	3	Users	Full time		

Step 5 (a) Put a margin for error in the plan

5(a).1 The idea

The plan that you've built as a result of applying steps 1-4 is your best prediction of how your project could unfold. In theory, at this point, you could deal with the constraints, but there's one other thing you must do before doing this. You must make the plan resilient by putting a margin for error into the plan. Without a margin for error, it's quite likely that your plan will fail the first time something unexpected happens on your project.

There are two ways to put a margin for error into the plan. One is to add in contingency. There are a number of ways to do this but in the subsection that follows we just describe one way. The other is to do risk analysis – attack the risks on your project before they attack you!

5(a).2 What to do

1. Add some additional time onto the end date of the project. This is to cover unexpected events that might occur over the life of the project. If you're looking for a rule of thumb then add 15% of the

duration of the project. In other words, if the project lasts 7 months, add an additional month for contingency.

2. Do a risk analysis of your project

    (i) Identify the risks to your project – those things that could cause the project to go wrong.

    (ii) Grade each risk as to how likely it is to happen. Use a scale of 1-3. 1= not very likely; 3 = highly likely; 2 = anything else. This is Likelihood.

    (iii) Grade each risk as to its Impact if it does happen. Use the same 1-3 scale.

    (iv) Multiply Likelihood by Impact to give Exposure.

    (v) For the high Exposure items (i.e. Exposure = 6 or 9), identify actions you can take to reduce these risks.

    (vi) Put these actions (i.e. jobs) into the plan and treat them just the same as any other jobs.

3. Go to step 5(b).

5(a).3 Example

See 5(a).2, (1) above for an example of contingency.

Here in Figure 6.5 is a sample risk analysis.

Figure 6.5 Sample of Risk Analysis

	Risks	Likelihood	Impact	LxI	Action
1	Poor management by company's executives	2	3	6	Performance review Training Quality assurance Strengthen management team
2	Under-resourcing	3	3	9	Verify targets against market data Hire more people Sort out Dance Cards of existing staff
3	Staff get sick	2	3	6	Shadowing Medicals for new employees Sort any existing problems
4	Lack of expertise	2	3	6	Training and development Proper and timely appraisals
5	Office space blow out	1	1	1	Begin looking for extra facilities
6	Competition	1	2	2	Continue competitor watch
7	Revenues don't happen – forecast is wrong	2	3	6	Weekly monitoring and change control Financial and mgmt. reports

Step 5(b) Manage peoples' expectations

5(b).1 The idea
A successful project is one where the stakeholders' expectations are set initially and then managed over the life of the project. To put it another way, your project will be successful if your project stakeholders always know how they stand. A major part of this is setting the stakeholders' expectations initially and that involves dealing with whatever constraints may have come with the project. The next section tells you what to do.

5(b).2 What to do
1. It may be that the dates, resource levels, budget and scope in your plan meet the constraints imposed by the stakeholders. In that case you can make commitments to the stakeholders based on your plan, i.e. you can tell them the end date, what the project will cost and what resources you need.
2. If (1) doesn't happen – and it rarely does! – then you can do the following. The version of the plan you have may not satisfy the constraints. But a revised version might. There are four variables connected with the plan that you can vary. These are:

*   What the project is delivering;
*   The delivery date;
*   The work involved/the budget;
*   The quality of what's being delivered.

3. By varying one or more of these it may be possible to come up with a version of the plan that satisfies the stakeholders.
4. If (2) doesn't happen, it means the stakeholders are asking for something that is impossible. YOU SHOULD ALWAYS DECLINE IMPOSSIBLE MISSIONS. Insist that the stakeholders only deal in reality, i.e. engage in (2) preceding. The stakeholders may not all be overjoyed at the end of the negotiation, but at least they know they can rely on what's being committed to, rather than being promised something which – in the fullness of time – turns out to have been impossible to do. Since this tends to be the key

issue in a lot of project management, all of Chapter 7 is devoted to this subject.

5. Now you're ready to begin executing the project. Once the commitments have been made to the stakeholders the project starts. The steps that follow are about executing the plan.

Step 6: Use an appropriate leadership style

6.1 The idea

A lot of your project management work is about getting people to do jobs for you. This is where your leadership style comes in. Everyone has a natural leadership style ranging from – at one end of the spectrum – hands-on, micromanagement to – at the other end – hands-off, leave-people-alone-to-get-on-with-it. Is one style better than another? Should you use one of the extremes or something in the middle? Should you be hands-off when things are going well and hands-on when they're not?

The next sub-section suggests what should be done in different situations. Obviously with people, each situation is unique, but section 6.2 offers some reference points from which you can make your own judgements.

6.2 What to do

1. Superstar. The person likes to do that particular job, has all the necessary skill and will almost certainly deliver. Leave them to get on with it with minimal sticking your nose in.

2. Solid citizen. The person is happy enough to do the job and knows how to do it. Maybe they don't get particularly fired up about doing it, but there's a pretty good chance they'll deliver. Don't get too much in their way, but neither assume it's all just going to happen.

3. Dodgy. For whatever reason – lack of motivation, lack of expertise, lack of time – there's a good chance this job isn't going to get done. Establish as quickly as you can whether it's going to happen or not. If it is, it becomes a 2, a Solid citizen; if not it becomes a 5, Goner.

4. Trainee. They're new to whatever it is. They're going to need hand holding, nurturing, mentoring, coaching, formal training,

micro-management before we can be confident they'll deliver.

5. Goner. It isn't going to happen. You need to find some other way of getting this job done. *And* you need to deal with the person. Your choices are anything on the spectrum from firing to rehabilitation.

Step 7 Know what's going on

7.1 The idea

The plan that you went to such trouble to develop has served two purposes already. First, it enabled you to understand the project in all its various aspects. Next it enabled you to make commitments that were achievable and stopped you from undertaking impossible missions. Here you see the third use of the plan as you use it as instrumentation to drive the project.

The tracking as described serves the following purposes:

- It ensures that the day to day shepherding the project forward gets done.
- It give a structure in which fire fights (unexpected events) can be handled.
- It ensures that big changes to the project are dealt with.
- It gives you a precise status check on the project.
- It enables the capturing of estimated versus actual data.

7.2 What to do

Do this every day:

1. Go down the plan from top to bottom and identify any job that requires some action by you today. These jobs are your to-do list.
2. Do these things.
3. Record in your plan actuals versus estimated, e.g. you said something would take 3 days, it actually took 5 days.
4. Record in your plan incidents, i.e. things that occurred on the project that the plan hadn't anticipated. Some incidents will be big changes (see section 1.1). These will require you to create a new

plan and to communicate that to the stakeholders. If they agree to this then this plan becomes the plan that you now work from. If not then the original plan stands.

5.   The other incidents will be handled either using your contingency – the best course of action – or by working more – not a good idea.

6.   From this updated version of the plan you can see the status of the project, i.e. has the end date changed, has the budget changed?

7.3 Example
Here's an example of actual versus estimated in Figure 6.6.

Figure 6.6 Example of actual vs estimated

ID	ⓞ	Task Name	Work	Duration	Actual Duration	02 Jun 03							09 Jun 03							16 Jun 03		
						M	T	W	T	F	S	S	M	T	W	T	F	S	S	M	T	W
1		**1 Project X**	**0 days**	**1 day**	**0 days**																	
6		**2 Users test the system**	**14 days**	**17 days**	**5 days**																	
7	✓	2.1 First test run	5 days	1 wk	1 wk												Charly - full time					
8		2.2 IT fix the errors	2 days	0.8 wks	0 wks																CI	
9		2.3 Second test tun	3 days	0.6 wks	0 wks																	
10		2.4 IT fix the errors	1 day	0.4 wks	0 wks																	
11		2.5 Final test run	3 days	0.6 wks	0 wks																	

Step 8: Tell people what's going on

8.1 The idea

Step 5(b) set the expectations of the stakeholders initially. Step (8) ensures that you continue to manage their expectations over the life of the project.

8.2 What to do
You know the status of the project from the preceding step. Once a week, communicate this to the stakeholders in a status report. There's an example as Figure 6.7 overleaf.

8.3 Example
Figure 6.7 Weekly status report

STATUS REPORT

Project:	Great Product Version 1.2
Report:	14
Date:	21 October 2010
Project Manager:	Frank
Team:	Rachel, Debbie, Declan, Steve, Mary
Distribution:	As above plus
	Bernadette, Hugh, Dan, Pedro, Ted,
	File + Tell anyone else who's interested

Overall Status:

Requirements	Design	Development	Testing	Limited customer release
Complete	Complete	Complete	In progress	Not yet started

Current dates are:

> Testing to complete on November 17 2010
> General availability (at end of limited customer release) –
> January 19 2011.

Delivery Date – change history

Date of Change	Reason for change	Into Beta date	General Availability date
	Original dates	1 May 2010	1 Sep 2010
9 May 1997	See section 1 of the Project Plan	24 Nov 2010	23 Jan 2011
27 May 1997	Added an extra person for a couple of weeks	12 Nov 2010	12 Jan 2011
2 July 1997	Some improvements due to use of Mary	3 Nov 2010	5 Jan 2011
14 Oct 1997	Slip in development schedule	17 Nov 2010	19 Jan 2011

Step 9: Repeat steps 1 through 8 until the project is over

9.1 The idea
You don't just have an orgy of planning and then take a giant jump to the end of the project. In reality you plan and then you move forward and then you re-plan. That's what the routine in section 7.2 describes. In doing so, notice that you end up going back through steps 1-8.

9.2 What to do
Nothing – you're already doing it!

Step 10: Do a post mortem or review on the project

10.1 The idea
Whether the project is an outstanding success, a monumental failure or anything in between, you want to learn something from it. This step is where you do that.

10.2 What to do

1. Be sure to gather input from as many stakeholders as possible.
2. Write down what you did well so you can do it again.
3. Write what was done badly, so you don't do it again.
4. Compare what you estimated in your plan with what actually happened. Use this information the next time you have to estimate and build a plan (see step 2).

How to Assess a Project in Five Minutes
This section describes how to assess a project in five minutes using the PSI (Probability of Success Indicator) that was mentioned briefly at the top of this chapter. The PSI is a measurement you can take at any point in a project's life and it tells you how likely or not the project is to succeed.

How is it measured?
The PSI is measured by rating the project against the criteria listed in Figure 6.8:

Figure 6.8 Criteria for PSI (Probability of Success Indicator)

Criterion	Available score
1. How well-defined or not is the goal	20
2. Is there a final, definitive detailed list of jobs where every job has been broken down to the 1-5 day level of detail?	20
3. Does the project have somebody who, day-to-day, shepherds all of the jobs forward?	10
4. Are there people to do all of the jobs identified in 2? Do those people have enough time availability to devote to the project?	10
5. Is there contingency in the plan?	5
6. Has an up-to-date risk analysis been done and are the jobs to reduce those risks part of the project plan?	5
7. How much does the project manager vary their management style with the circumstances, micro-managing where necessary and hands-off in other situations?	10
8. Is the project tracked on a regular basis? Never = 0; Daily = 10	10
9. Is there weekly *meaningful* status reporting?	10
Total	**100**

How to calculate the PSI

1. This is a measure of how well-defined the goal is. The acid test here is that if you were to ask each stakeholder what the goal of the project is, and if each were to give you almost exactly the same reply, then the goal is well-defined. Otherwise it is not. You only get a 20 when the project is complete because only then do you know exactly what was achieved. A project which is at a very early stage and where the goal has yet to be nailed down, would

score low. A project where the goal had been reasonably well clarified, but agreement is still needed from some of the stakeholders would get a medium/in-the-middle sort of score. Pick a number between 0 and 20.

2. This is a measure of how complete the list of jobs is. Zero is no list. You might get 2 or 3 for a high level Work Breakdown Structure i.e. just the big phases. You only get 20 when the project completes because only then do you know exactly what the list of jobs was. Pick a number between 0 and 20. If the goal (Step 1) scores low, then this will score low, since, if you won't know what you're trying to do, how could you have a list of jobs to do it?

3. If the leader can be named and that person has adequate time available to run the project, then give 10, otherwise give 0.

4. If there aren't any/enough people to do the work, score this 0 or low. Also take into account that this step should be in the same proportion as Step 2, e.g. a 14/20 for Step 2 would give at most a 7/10 for Step 4.

5. Allocate the 10 in two 5s. The first 5 is for contingency. The more contingency, the higher the score out of 5.

6. The second 5 is for how well or badly the risk reducing activities have been identified and are being carried out. For a project with lots of level 6 and level 9 risks (i.e. a high-risk project) score low; for projects with few 9s and 6s (i.e. a low-risk project), score high.

7. Pick a number between 0 and 10 based on how well the project manager varies their management style with the circumstances.

8. Pick a number between 0 and 10 based on how well the project manager uses the plan to steer the project. If the plan was thrown away as soon as the project was given the green light, score 0.

9. Pick a number between 0 and 10 based upon the regularity and adequacy of status reports.

How to interpret PSIs

(1) If the goal isn't right, nothing will be right

If the goal isn't right, you miss one of the two opportunities to get a high score, but notice how it all unravels. If you don't know what you're trying to do, creating a list of jobs to do it is impossible. (So too, it's worth noting, is setting the expectations of the stakeholders. If you don't know what you're trying to do, how could you set them? What will happen is that everyone will set his or her own expectations.) Thus the list is flawed resulting in missing the other opportunity to get a high score. If the list is flawed then shepherding the project forward (3) is impossible, as is assigning people to the jobs (4). Contingency (5) and risk analysis (6) will have no meaning. 7 and 8 both require the job list and so a flawed job list causes these to fall apart as well.

(2) 60 is an important threshold
A PSI should start off low and rise steadily over the life of the project. Initially projects may not score more than 60, and this can just mean that there is more work to be done in terms of scoping the project (1) and planning it (2 through 6). However, a project should quickly go above 60 and stay above it. (Notice that the latter isn't guaranteed, and a project can drop back again. This could happen, for example, if a big change to the scope of the project went uncontrolled.)

(3) Low scores always point you at the priority problem areas
Which is nice, I think you'll agree.

(4) You can do anything you like on a poorly planned project and it won't make the blindest bit of difference
We mentioned already (in Chapter 2) Brooks' Law – "adding people to a late project makes it later". I believe that the above statement – "you can do anything you like ..." – can be viewed as a generalisation of Brooks' Law. It basically says that if your project gets into difficulties, go back and look at the plan; don't just, for example, blindly ask everyone to work harder. The problem is in the plan, not in the execution of the plan.

Example of assessing a PSI
The following is based on a real project. Suppose you were faced with this problem: a project which is scheduled to take 17 months has been running for 11. There are about 250 people working on it. The project is very significant to the organisation and so a very senior person has been

given the job of running it. There is lots of activity on the project. People are working long hours. Is the project in good shape or not?

Using your PSI checklist to guide you in your investigation you uncover the status given in column three of the following table (Figure 6.9). You then score the project as described in column four.

Figure 6.9 Example of PSI scorecard

Criterion	Available score	Status	Actual score
1. How well-defined or not is the goal	20	Specifications for much of the project still don't exist even though the project is due to end in 6 months	Based on the proportion of specifications completed to those still not done, you score the project 14
2. Is there a final, definitive detailed list of jobs where every job has been broken down to the 1-5 day level of detail?	20	Some parts of the project have plans, some parts have no plans. The bits that haven't been specified have no plans	Since only 70% (14/20) of the project is defined, this is the most that this could score. A 70% would be possible if all of the bits of the project that were specified had plans. However, some don't. Score this 10
3. Does the project have somebody who, day-to-day, shepherds all of the jobs forward?	10	The very senior person still has all their other responsibilities, so they don't give anywhere near enough time to	This project doesn't have a leader. It has somebody with the title but nobody doing the job. Score 0

		devote to a project of this magnitude. In addition, they see the day-to-day shepherding of the project as work that is below them	
4. Are there people to do all of jobs identified in in 2? Do those people have enough time availability to devote to the project?	10	See 2	Since only 50% (10/20) of the jobs are identified, this could score no more than 50%. Give it 5
5. Is there contingency in the plan?	5	No.	Score 0
6. Has an up-to-date risk analysis been done and are the jobs to reduce those risks part of the project plan?	5	No.	Score 0
7. How much does the project manager vary their management style with the circumstances,	10	See 3	Score 0

micro-managing where necessary and hands-off in other situations ?			
8. Is the project tracked on a regular basis? Never = 0; Daily = 10	10	See 3	Score 0
9. Is there weekly *meaningful* status reporting?	10	See 2, 3 and 8	Since there is no proper plan, status reporting has no meaning. Score 0
Total	**100**		**29**

Conclusion?

The project is two-thirds of the way through its planned life and yet its PSI is well below 60. The project is in disastrous shape and is going nowhere. It has no chance of succeeding in its current form and will seriously overshoot its budget and its deadline.

To rescue this project, the following need to be done in the order indicated:

1. Re-plan the project. (By including contingency in the plan and doing a risk analysis, scores 5 and 6 will both climb).
2. Use the plan to reset the expectations of the stakeholders. (This will not be a pleasant exercise.)
3. Complete the specifications. This will cause the 14/20 score to climb.
4. With the goal specified it will be possible to finalise the detailed

list of jobs (causing the 10/20 to climb).

5.   Now people will be working on the right things and everything else should start falling into place.

Chapter 7

How To Say No To An Impossible Project

The single biggest reason why projects fail is that they were never actually possible in the first place. Somebody said, "Here's the project, it has to be done by this date, for this budget with these resources", and everybody just said "OK". Being offered impossible projects is a fact of life, sure. But always saying yes to them doesn't have to be a fact of life. When you're given impossible projects there are smarter things you can do than just saying "OK". They're smarter for you as the project manager, smarter for your team and smarter for the other project stakeholders.

This chapter tells you what to do when faced with an impossible project. It describes strategies that will enable you to successfully execute such projects to the delight of the stakeholders.

How to properly recognise an impossible project
I described in the previous chapter how when projects are handed to us they almost always come with constraints – wishes that the stakeholders have about how and when the project should be done.

If we do our job properly as project managers then the first thing we do is to build a realistic plan for the project, as described in the previous chapter. Once we have done that, if the plan says that the constraints are unachievable, i.e. some or all of the date/budget/resource/scope constraints cannot be achieved, then the project we have been given is impossible.

Notice here the importance of the plan. If there is no proper plan – by "proper" I mean properly estimated – then there can be no impossible project. The project may look impossible, smell impossible, people may be using that terrifying phrase,"This is a very aggressive schedule", but without a properly estimated plan there is no objective measure of whether or not the project is indeed impossible.

However, assuming that you have indeed been handed an impossible project, then the rest of this chapter tells you how to deal with the unexploded bomb in your hands.

What to do with an impossible project

The realistic plan that you built – the one that enabled you to diagnose whether or not the project was impossible – is also your tool for dealing with the impossible project. That plan involves four very important variables or parameters. These are:

- What (the project is delivering).
- When (the project is delivering it).
- Work. The amount of work involved in getting the project done. (Notice that this, in turn, gives you the budget of the project.)
- Quality. There are a whole bunch of jobs or tasks in the plan whose purpose is to ensure the quality of the finished product. (Typically, these are things like reviews, testing, quality assurance, walkthroughs, signoffs and so on).

You will use these four parameters to help you deal with your impossible project.

When you have an impossible project, you basically have a version of the plan that the stakeholders don't find acceptable. It's like you have a vanilla plan, but the stakeholders don't like vanilla. But that's no problem, you can build other flavours. By varying the four parameters you can come up with other flavours of the plan that the stakeholders may like. And not only that, the stakeholders can ask about certain flavours and you can see if we can make those flavours.

It's important, however, for everybody to realise that your plan (your ice cream machine!) is not infinitely variable. There are certain flavours that it may not be able to make. If that is the case you need to tell that to the stakeholders and stop them from choosing an impossible flavour. Here's how you can vary the four parameters.

WHAT

You can "de-scope' the project. You can do less. If you have categorised what the project is delivering into "have to haves" and "nice to haves", then maybe you can just deliver the "have to haves". Maybe you can reconsider what you actually regard as "have to have", i.e. you do the categorisation again. You can explore with the stakeholders whether it is possible to deliver the project in some sort of increments rather than all at once.

WHEN

You can try to understand the significance of the constraints date you've been given. Some dates are inherently suspect:

- 24 December (or really, any date in the approximate range 20 December – 3 January or so, i.e. the Christmas period). I accept that for some projects, e.g. the changeover to the Euro, the 31st December date had huge significance. But for many projects these end of year dates are nothing more than the yearning of some tidy-minded person somewhere wanting the project to be over. (I accept also that this may be somewhat different in the U.S. where Christmas holidays are generally not so long).
- Check what day of the week the constraints date falls on. If it's a Saturday, a Sunday or a public holiday then, once again, it may not have any real significance. It often means that nobody has actually thought out why the end date is important. When you force them to do that it may buy you some extra time. (Once again, I accept that weekend dates can have a huge significance, i.e. they can be to do with taking live systems down, for example, and replacing or upgrading them. It's still worth asking, though.)
- In some countries, some months are holiday months e.g. August in France or July in Sweden, so often – again, not always – a constraints date occurring in these months may not be a real date, or there may be some 'give' in it.
- Finally, the constraints date may be to do with your stakeholders

wanting to carve out some contingency for themselves. For instance, they need the thing done by say, 31 August, but they've told you 10 August. Thus, if you slip, they'll still have a good chance of being on time. So, in this example, August 31 may actually be the real constraints date.

Probing these things doesn't always help – but it certainly can't hurt.

WORK
You can look and see what the effect of adding more people to the project will be. Don't forget Brooks' Law though, ("Adding people to a late project makes it later"). Make sure that adding these extra people won't have:

- Little effect
- No effect
- A negative effect.

On the other hand, it may be possible to parachute in specialists who'll be able to hit the ground running and will need very little by way of a learning curve. In that case, you may indeed be able to, say, shorten the project and bring a plan date closer to a constraints date.

QUALITY
Finally, of course you don't compromise on quality, but maybe you can reduce the amount of testing or QA you had planned to do and still have something that the stakeholders will be happy with. Or – more promising – can you get reviews and sign-offs done quicker? Can people – especially stakeholders – turn things around quicker, get you decisions faster, so that you can gain some precious days and make the plan date and the constraints date converge?

By varying some or all of these four parameters, as I have described, you can come up with alternative versions of the plan, and you should be able to convince the stakeholders that their best chance lies with one of these. Equally you should be able to discourage stakeholders from choosing a course of action which your plan says cannot be achieved and is doomed to failure.

This is your first, most important and most promising strategy. It should be possible to solve all constraints type problems in this way. If people are of good will and want the best for the project, then this is how these situations should always be handled. Stakeholders asking for impossible courses of action should be told politely but firmly that what they are asking for is not a runner. The plan and the facts in it – and only these – should be used as the basis for any discussion and agreement. Anyone engaging in bullying, unreasonable behaviour or trying to pretend there isn't a problem ("So, we're all agreed then – the date's achievable?")should be pulled back gently to the plan and told to consider the facts.

The Flexibility Matrix
A particularly useful idea when trying to either (a) generate flavours or (b) get stakeholders to pick one is to get stakeholders to fill in what's known as a flexibility matrix. This enables you to understand what's important to them. Figure 7.1 offers an example of one.

Figure 7.1 Example of a flexibility matrix

	High	Medium	Low
Scope		x	
Deadline	x		
Resources			X

This particular flexibility matrix assumes that the stakeholders don't want to mess with quality but are prepared to look at the other three parameters – What (Scope), When (Deadline), Work (Resources). In this example, the stakeholders have said they are very flexible on the deadline, less flexible on the scope and not really flexible at all on the resources. (The important rule here obviously is that stakeholders can only put one 'x' in each row and each column!) Thus, if you were trying to come up with a flavour that would satisfy these stakeholders, they would be far less likely to accept one that required extra resources than they would to accept one where the deadline moved or the project scope was reduced.

What if they question your estimates?

You have one weak point in all this and canny stakeholders may spot it. They will say to you, "But these are just estimates – they could be all wrong, and it could be that my estimates are correct and that the project is very doable". It's a tough argument to deal with, but it *can* be dealt with. Here's what you do.

You say that you accept that these are estimates and that they could be wrong. You believe that the level of detail coupled with the contingency and risk analysis gives you a high level of confidence in them, but, yes, they could be wrong. It's worth pointing out to them too that the estimates could be wrong, but not in the way that the stakeholders are suggesting. The estimates could be *under*-estimates, i.e. things could actually be much worse than even what your plan says. But, yes, you accept that that you could have over-estimated everything and the project could be possible.

So here's what you agree. You agree to run the project for a few weeks and record what actually happens. On a date (that you agree now) you will meet and compare the actuals against the estimates. If the actuals come in very much less than the estimates then they were right. If the actuals come in very close to the estimates then you were right. You get agreement from them that in the latter situation, they will then accept your plan.

What about 'voicing your concerns'?

This is the tactic whereby the project manager believes the project can't be done, but agrees to do it on condition that he gets to "voice his concerns", i.e. write a memo stating that, in his view, the project is impossible. Does this work?

In my opinion it doesn't. As far as the stakeholders are concerned, the project manager has accepted the project. The stakeholders will happily file the "cover-your-ass" memo in a place where it will never be found again. They will either never read it or promptly forget its contents. And when the project does run into trouble – as it almost inevitably will – the project manager pathetically waving his memo in the air will cut a sorry figure. He will also, without doubt, be blamed for the fiasco.

What if all this doesn't work?

If the approaches described previously don't work with your stakeholders then you need stronger medicine. This is described in the next section.

Extreme Survival Skills

Sometimes you end up dealing with situations or with stakeholders where reason no longer prevails. You may hear many of the phrases I have spoken of earlier:

- "Saying no is not an option"; or
- "I'm sorry – we just have to do it"; or
- "Sure, it's an aggressive schedule, but I'm sure you'll find a way"; or
- "The problem with you is that you're far too negative"; or
- "You're going to have to learn to be more flexible"; or
- "That's not the culture around here"; or
- "We need can-do people here"; or
- "Don't bring me problems, bring me solutions"; or
- "Is this plan based on a 5 day week?"; or
- "If you don't do it, I'll find somebody who will";

    or much worse things.

Sometimes – it has to be said – this pressure to take on an impossible project may not come from external sources at all. You may generate it yourself. You may want to show that you have the right stuff, that you have what it takes. As a result, when somebody says, "This is a very aggressive schedule", some macho thing within you takes over, you draw yourself up to your full height and say "This is the hour; I am the man (or woman)."

Whether the pressure comes internally or externally, if you find yourself under this pressure, what you *should* do is to say "no" – decline the impossible project.

What happens if you don't do this is described in the next section. Different ways of saying "no" – these are our "extreme survival skills" – are described after that.

What happens if you say "yes" to an impossible project

If you say "yes" to an impossible project, then sometimes your efforts result in monumental disasters. But sometimes – incredibly – you pull them off. You take something that everybody said was impossible and you manage to get it done.

If you do this, if you manage to pull off an impossible mission, then you join a very select club that is called the Magicians Club. Magicians do exactly as the name suggests. They do magic tricks. They take things which look as though they can't be done and make them happen.

In a sense, we can't say enough good things about Magicians. They provide an astonishing level of service. They do magic tricks. They take impossible things and they make them happen. Imagine you went to an interview and the interviewer asked "What do you do?" and you replied "I do impossible missions". They'd hand you the contract and say "How much do we have to pay you?"

There are other good things you can say about Magicians. It's true to say that not everybody in the organisation is a Magician. We'd all have to nod our heads on that one. And, so, organisations should love their Magicians. Bring them flowers and champagne. Give them bonuses and stock options and salary rises and company cars and all the rest of it. Love them to death.

But there is a problem with being a Magician that we need to talk about. There is a dark secret at the heart of being a Magician. It's probably best illustrated by the graph shown as Figure 7.2:

Figure 7.2 The Magician's secret

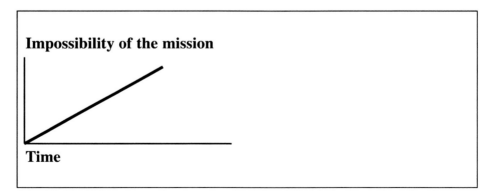

On the horizontal axis is time. On the vertical one is the how impossible the mission is. On the low end of the scale, the mission is only mildly impossible, i.e. the gap between the supply and the demand is relatively small. On the high end, everybody's completely lost the plot – there's an enormous gap between the supply and the demand. So, as with all Magicians, your career starts out on the low end of the scale. You begin by doing low-grade tricks.

So try and imagine now that you're in a theatre. In the front row, just beyond the footlights, you can see all of your stakeholders. There's your boss, your boss's boss, there's your team, your colleagues and co-workers, your customers, and so on. Now, you walk on stage in your Magician's costume, and, right before their eyes, you pull a rabbit from the hat. And the audience goes wild. They're applauding, cheering, whistling, stamping their feet. Your boss is nudging your boss's boss and saying,"That's my Magician. I hired him/her. Isn't (s)he wonderful?" Your team are saying, "S(he) led us to victory". It's a sweet moment. If you've ever had one, and I'm sure you have, you'll know just how sweet it can be.

Now the next time you go on stage, a rabbit from the hat really isn't going to impress anybody. But that's OK. Encouraged by your success, you'll try a bigger animal. Little dogs to begin with. Poodles. And then bigger dogs. German Shepherds. And then a very big dog indeed. An Irish Wolfhound. And that probably does it with canines. You move on to equines. Mules, donkeys, ponies, racehorses, show jumpers. Then – relentlessly – giraffes, hippopotamuses, rhinoceros, elephants. If you stay at this long enough, you'll eventually pull the biggest mammal on Earth from the hat. The blue whale. All one hundred and fifty tons of it, pulled – excruciatingly – from the hat.

And while most of the stakeholders are still delighted – overwhelmed, indeed, at the scale of your achievement – there are some who aren't quite as perky as they were when all this began. Your team, for example, is exhausted, having just endured another "death march" project [4]. And for the first time, you notice some stakeholders that you hadn't really paid much attention to before. They're in the second row and they're the husbands, wives, children, lovers, boyfriends, girlfriends, brothers, sisters, parents, pets – those people that love us and like to see us occasionally. They're not looking particularly happy as your

Magician performances mean that you spend less and less time with them.

You would think that when you'd done the blue whale, you could stop. You would think that the company would put up a little plaque on your office door or cubicle wall. It would say "This is Charly's office. She pulled the blue whale from the hat. Tread softly as you walk by." You would have a sort of honorary retirement, and people would come and gaze in at you as the person who had achieved so much.

Of course, nothing could be further from the truth. If you've done the blue whale, then the stakeholders will just look for a more spectacular trick. Given that there are no bigger mammals to pull from hats, you turn your attention to sawing the lady in half. (I'm assuming you know this trick. There's a large rectangular box, a bit like a big coffin. A woman lies in it. Her head sticks out a hole at one end and her feet stick out two holes at the other. The magician takes a saw and saws the box down the centre. Then he separates the two pieces of the box. The woman's head and torso are in one section of the box and they appear to be separated from her legs and feet, which are in the other.)

And so you start sawing ladies in half. And the stakeholders are stunned. They thought they'd seen it all with mammals from hats, but this has brought your magicianship to a whole other level.

Except that, one night you go on stage, you put the lady in the box, you start the chainsaw, you saw down the centre of the box and fountains of blood come out everywhere. The trick goes horribly wrong. You take on a supply-demand imbalance that can't actually be closed. (After all, there *are* only 24 hours in a day.) And it's a terrible moment. It's a terrible, terrible moment. It's particularly terrible for your team, who have worked so hard only to see the whole thing go horribly wrong. It's terrible for the stakeholders. They hadn't been expecting this. And sometimes the retribution can be terrible.

What happens to Magicians after that? Well, for a while, they may stay in that organisation. They may continue to go on stage. But when they do, the confidence of former times is replaced by terror. You don't know, the stakeholders don't know, the lady in the box doesn't know, what's going to happen when you start the chainsaw. Almost inevitably, the haggard, stumbling figure of the burnt-out (for such they are) Magician moves on. They go to a new company or organisation. They start out low on the scale again, with low-grade tricks, pulling rabbits and other little creatures from hats. But it's only a matter of time before they replay the whole scenario we've already described and end up in the same place.

So, to use a popular word, the dark heart of being a Magician is that it is *unsustainable*. It may have some short-term benefits – to the team, your colleagues, your boss, your company, your customers. Long-term, it has no benefits to anybody. This is what happens if you habitually say "yes" to impossible missions. If you find yourself being pressurised to take on an impossible mission, and none of the preceding has worked, then there are a range of other solutions available to you. They are described in turn.

Other tactics

Before I begin this section just let me state yet again that these impossible mission situations – no matter how difficult or unpleasant they are – should really be resolved using the "options" technique as described earlier in the chapter.

However, if that hasn't worked for you, here are a number of more desperate remedies that will also fix the problem, and by "fix" I mean fix it to the satisfaction of all the stakeholders. To put it another way, the tactics which follow will help you to make a *wise* decision.

You could say "yes"

In certain circumstances saying "yes" may be a wise decision. This may sound like I'm contradicting my previous advice, but I'm not. There's a difference between saying "yes" on a one-off basis and doing it always. You could possibly choose this tactic if the gap between what the plan says is possible and what the constraints say is necessary was not too great. Suppose you did cancel vacations, work weekends and late nights. If you factored all that additional effort into the plan, would that make things come right? (Notice again that you're using the plan to guide you.)

If the answer is no, then you need to look at one of the other three tactics which follow.

However, if the answer is yes, you then need to go and say to your team, "What about it team?" If they're not up for this, then you need to move on to one of the tactics which follow. If they are, then maybe you want to go back and say "yes" to your stakeholders. But be conscious of everything we said in the section about being a Magician. If this project works out, what will your stakeholders expect after this?

But if this is truly a once-off, in these very specific circumstances:

- Very definitely a once-off project; and
- Gap between plan and constraints bridgeable; and
- Team up for it.

then saying "yes" may constitute a wise decision.

You could say "no"
It may be that everyone has completely lost the plot, i.e. that the gap between what the plan says is possible and what the constraints says is necessary is so great that it could never be bridged.

In that case, you want to get a million miles away from the project because when the bomb goes off here, the mess is going to be appalling. You want to document your reasons for passing on the project. You can add to your document your prediction of what you believe is going to happen (based on the plan), i.e. the mess that is going to be created if this plan is committed to in its current form. Finally, if you really want to rub it in, you can use your plan to say here's how that mess will have to be sorted out when the time comes. All of this should give your stakeholders major cause for thought. In my experience, it has often – though not always – been enough to bring stakeholders around to your point of view.

For you, in these circumstances, saying "no" might constitute a wise decision.

You could play the "big change" game
In construction, where the lowest bidder often gets the job, they do this all the time – and highly successfully. (Maybe you know some owners of construction companies who are poor. I have to say I don't know any.)

Let's say that your plan says that the project is going to cost euros/$/£ 500 K and the stakeholders say, you have to do it for euros/$/£ 350K. An impossible mission.

You say "Sure, I'll take it for three fifty".
Now – every time the stakeholders make the teeny weeniest change to
what they asked for, you slap them with a "big change" and you change
the plan (date, work, budget) accordingly. In addition, you use slips on
the stakeholder side to mask any slips on your side.

It could well be that by using this tactic, you take an impossible
project and manage your way to making it possible. Construction
projects do this routinely.

You could accept the project but not the constraints
A neat trick. Here's how it works. Let's say you have a project where
the constraints date is 6 September, but the plan says 29 November. An
impossible mission.

Now, as we mentioned earlier, you have that one weakness in all of
this – a weakness upon which the stakeholders may pounce. "Ah-ha",
they may say, "your plan is a prediction and so it could be all wrong.
You could have over-estimated everything and this project could be
very do-able".

"It could be," you agree reasonably. "I could have under-estimated
everything too, of course, so that the situation could be far worse than
I've said here. But here's what I'm prepared to do. I'll give it a try and
here's what I guarantee. I don't believe 6 September is possible so I
can't guarantee that. I *can* guarantee 29 November . But what I'll also
do for you is that every week I'll tell you how we're doing".

The stakeholders will always accept this. What they've heard is the
sound of you getting into your Magician's costume. What they believe
you said was that you would give the project a try – or, in other words,
you're going to have a crack at 6 September.

Now, this is not what you said. So you need to start reminding them.
The first week of the project you issue a status report, as in Figure 7.3.

Figure 7.3 First week's project status report

Here's what you asked for:	September 6
Here's what we're committed to:	November 29
Here's what our plan is saying today:	November 29 (It'd be a pretty bad plan if you couldn't keep it on target for the first week!)

You continue to do this every week. During this time your stakeholders will go through a period of denial where they're not listening to what you're saying. So, as well as writing the status report, you need to be bending their ear – we're probably talking primarily about your boss here – and saying "What are *you* going to do about this 6 September/29 November problem". The "you" is a very important word here. This is their problem – not yours. You never committed to 6 September. They did.

You keep doing this until they hear you. Then they may go into a period of irrational behaviour where they start repeating a lot of the phrases we've mentioned several times in this book. However, you continue to beam out the same message, as in Figure 7.4:

Figure 7.4 Continuing Status Reports

Here's what you asked for:	September 6
Here's what we're committed to:	November 29
Here's what our plan is saying today:	We'd like to think it'd be on or before November 29!

Finally, if you just stick to your guns and keep beaming out the status reports, they will eventually pass into the third phase where they wake up and smell the coffee and start to deal with the 6 September/29 November issue.

It's worth saying that this tactic prolongs a negotiation that really should have been resolved with the "options" approach. But needs must. This tactic will give you a wise decision – especially if you have one/a group of extremely volatile, disagreeable or dysfunctional stakeholders.

Notice that this tactic will also work if the stakeholders renege on the agreement to review the project described in the section above called "What if they question your estimates?".

PART TWO
Chapter 8

Step 1: Measure Where You Are

The first step in installing a Zero Waste system is to figure out where you are at the moment – to get some kind of reading about what kind of shape your organisation is in.

To do that there are four things you must do:

1. Decide what period of time you want to look at.
2. Make a list of all the projects you are doing or plan to do over that period.
3. Figure out the status of each project. This will use a scheme that is described below.
4. Calculate what is called the Organisational Performance Indicator (OPI).

Happily, doing this work isn't just about getting this reading. This is also the foundation upon which the rest of your Zero Waste work will be built. This chapter tells you what to do and begins the worked example which will run throughout the rest of the book.

(1) Decide what period of time you want to look at

What you are going to do in the next few chapters is going to fundamentally change the way you run your organisation. So, in terms of its importance and its effect on the organisation, it is probably comparable to when you do your strategic planning for the year. For that reason then, it probably makes sense to use the same kind of period of time that you would use if you were doing strategic planning. Thus – and this is just a suggestion – if you were doing this Zero Waste work in January through May of a particular year, you might want to look at the period from where you are now to the end of that year. If you were doing the Zero Waste work in June through December, you might want to consider looking at the rest of that year and the following year.

(2) Make a list of all of the projects

You need to identify all of the projects you are doing or plan to do over that period. This will include three types of projects:

- Known and committed projects. Projects that you know about and to which the organisation is committed.
- "I didn't know we were doing that" projects. Projects that somehow came into life and are currently being worked on. The reason why they are in existence may not be 100% clear; nor may it be clear who authorised them or how they came to life. But, somewhere along the way, somebody committed something to somebody so that now you have to take this into account.
- Future projects. You're going to have to make some attempt to predict what projects you might have to do over the period of time in question. The things you learned about estimating in Chapter 5 will enable you to do this.

Now obviously for a very large organisation there could be hundreds and hundreds of projects. So, if this is your first time trying all of this, you may want to reduce the size of the organisation you are looking at, e.g. rather than looking at a whole company you might want to look at just one division or group or section.

Known and committed projects
This should be the easiest part of the procedure. You need to make a list of all the projects that the organisation is involved in and committed to

at the moment. Maybe the list already exists and gets reported on every week. Or maybe there's no list but everybody knows (or thinks they do!). Or maybe you're not 100% sure. In that case, get the people together who do know and make the list. You just want a list at this stage. No calculations or anything else – just the names of the projects.

"I didn't know we were doing that" projects

These projects may well not appear on any list – at least not any central, consolidated, organisation-wide one. These are the projects that just somehow got started – maybe nobody's 100% sure exactly how. Maybe the boss (or somebody) just came in one day and said, "Forget everything else, I've got a really great idea" or "maybe we could just investigate this" or "don't spend too much time on this but …" Or maybe there's some maverick in the organisation somewhere responsible for it. In a sense it doesn't matter – at least, for now it doesn't. For now what matters is that somebody has committed something to somebody. (If that second somebody is one of your organisation's customers, then that makes the commitment especially serious.) For now, though, you just need to get its name onto your list.

Future projects

In general you won't know for sure everything you're going to do in the future. Some projects will depend on whether you win certain business or get certain customer orders. Whether you go ahead with some projects or not will depend on the business climate at the time. You can only make some kind of prediction or best guess now. So what you're going to do is to do exactly that – make a prediction; in other words, an estimate as described in Chapter 5. To do this you're going to make some assumptions – your best guess – about which projects are going to happen over the period that you're looking at.

(3) Figure out the status of each project

Next you need to identify the status of each project. For now, you will do that with what I call a "soft audit". Later on we will look at the more definitive way to do it.

A soft audit is the simplest, quickest and least-threatening way (to the person whose project is being audited) to assess the health of a project. All you do is ask the project manager what the status is and whatever s(he) says you take as gospel. Each project is then given one of the following four statuses:

- Green (which gets a score of 5). The project has a written plan and is running to plan.
- Amber (score of 3). The project has a written plan but has run into some problems. The project manager is addressing them and expects to bring the project back to green.
- Blue (scores 0). The project has no written plan.
- Red (scores -1). Whether the project had a written plan or not, it is now out of control.

So, in detail then:

1. Does the project have a written plan? (You don't even have to ask to see it). If they say yes, then go to question 2. Otherwise this is a Blue (0).
2. Is the project on target? If the Project Manager says yes, then you just take his/her word for it. The project is Green (5). If the answer is no, go to question 3.
3. How much is the project off target? If the answer is to the effect of "a little but we can/are taking steps to rectify it", then this is an Amber (3). If the answer is to the effect of "very much" then this is a Red (-1).

Now enter these scores beside your list of projects.

It's perhaps worth saying at this point that, in reality, things rarely turn out as rosily as this picture generally shows:

- Often Greens (on target) are not really. The plan was never accurate in the first place, is out of date or is not being tracked against properly. Or all three!
- Ambers (some problems) are really Reds. The "some problems which could be fixed" are actually huge problems which are going to require a fundamental re-planning of the project.

- Greens and Ambers are often Blues. The plan – such as it is – isn't actually worth the paper it's written on.

However, you don't need to worry about this for the moment. You'll deal with all of that in due course. What you *do* need to start thinking about though is that any projects which are either Blue (no written plan) or Red (out of control) should be considered as being "At Risk". There is definitely major waste occurring in these.

(4) Calculate the Organisational Performance Indicator (OPI)

You can think of the OPI as a description of the organisation. It is a description not in terms of its mission statement, or its balance sheet, or its strategic plan, or its business plan, or its organisation chart, or the market sectors it services, or any of the million-and-one others ways you could describe an organisation. Rather the organisation is defined in terms of the projects it is running. In other words, we want to define the organisation to be the sum of its projects.

To calculate the OPI, add up the individual scores of all the projects and divide the result by the total number of projects. The resulting number is a number between -1 and 5. The closer to -1 you are, the worse the shape in which your projects – and hence your organisation – are. The closer you are to 5, the better their shape. A score of 5 would mean that all your projects had been planned properly and were running to plan. (Not an impossible idea, in case you were thinking otherwise.)

You'll see below that the OPI and associated project status chart give you – at a glance – a lot of incredibly useful information.

The Worked Example – The Acme Company

To make the Zero Waste method as real as possible to you, and also to provide you with templates upon which you can base your own work, a worked example runs throughout the remainder of the book. This example concerns a (hypothetical) organisation that develops technology products. (We don't need to be any more precise than that). The company is called the Acme Company and employs just under 40 people but plans to grow to nearly 50 within the next 18 months. (I have chosen an organisation of this size only to keep the worked example to manageable proportions. At the end of each chapter I will mention briefly how this example could be scaled up or down.)

Basically, the organisation has a side that brings in business (Sales & Marketing) and a side that delivers the business (Product Development). This is what the organisation is like in terms of numbers of people:

There is a CEO, a Finance person, a person and two admin staff. In Sales & Marketing, there is a Head of Sales, three salespeople, a Marketing person and an admin person. In Product Development, there is a Head of Product Development, three Team Leaders/Section Managers and 19 Development Engineers. Product Support, which looks after customers, takes support calls, does installation and training, consists of 3 people.

The Acme Company – "Acme", for short – has been in business for about five years. It has clients in several European countries. It went through a couple of loss-making years as it was starting up, but for the last three years has made a profit. This profit has been reinvested into the company to continue it to grow. It makes standard products and also does "specials" – custom versions of its products for certain customers.

At the time that Acme decides to begin its Zero Waste work, there are some problems in the organisation. Sales & Marketing, which feels it's pretty good at what it does, has brought in lots of business. However, it constantly complains that Product Development essentially can't keep pace with them. Sales & Marketing brings the business in, Product Development makes commitments but then, rarely if ever, delivers on those commitments. Often too, if it does deliver on commitments, it is only after major heroics of working nights and weekends, with Sales & Marketing not knowing, right up to the last minute, whether or not the customer is going to get what was promised.

Product Development also feels it's pretty good at what it does. After all, they're the people who manage to pull off the impossible missions that Sales & Marketing keeps handing them. Apart from the problem of impossible missions, Product Development constantly accuses Sales & Marketing of "changing their minds all the time". Sales & Marketing has a different view of this. It sees this as "doing whatever is necessary to win the business and keep the customer happy".

Everybody's working long hours. Product Development is doing so for the reasons just cited. Sales & Marketing is doing so because it's hungry for business but also because its customer base is European-wide, so Sales & Marketing people spend a lot of time on the road. It's always been like this in Acme, right from the time it started. During its first three or four years everybody was prepared to work the long hours on the basis that they were in start-up mode, and that that's just the way things are in a start-up. But now, as the company enters its sixth year of being in business, people's enthusiasm and resilience is flagging a bit. They're wondering if it is always going to be like this.

Unfortunately, it's not the nineties any longer when, if people felt like this, they could just walk down the street and get another job on a higher salary. The Recession has come and so, if anybody complains, it is hinted (or they are told straight out) that they're lucky to have a job. People kind of know this anyway, but it doesn't help to be told. In short, morale isn't what it used to be.

The CEO is an enlightened man and has been wondering for some time if there is a better way. He's bought the book you're holding in your hand and he's going to give it a shot.

Worked Example – Step 1: Measure Where You Are

(1) Decide what period of time you want to look at

It is 1 July as the CEO decides to try out Zero Waste. Given that, with summer holidays and everything, July and August are a bit of a washout and after that that there are only four months in the year (September – December), he decides to look at a period from now until the end of the following year. In total then, he is going to look at a period of 18 months, 1 July of this year through to 31 December of next year. (As we said earlier, the choice is completely arbitrary.)

(2) Make a list of all of the projects

The CEO gets a status report every week from the Head of Product Development which lists all of the projects and says what their status is. He uses this as a start point. But then, he checks with the Head of Sales & Marketing to find out whether this is the definitive list. He shows the Head of Sales & Marketing the list and asks him "Can you think of any other project or product that is not on here that has been promised to customers in some way, shape or form?"

"Nope, that looks like it," says the Head of Sales & Marketing.

Then, after a pause, he adds, "except for the so-and-so. I don't see that on there. And, of course, customer X is looking for the whats-its-name. We said we would do that for them. And I don't know if when it says Product Y on that list, they mean the three different variants of Product Y. You should maybe check that."

Just to be doubly on the safe side, the CEO suggests they call in the three sales people to see if they have any more things like this. In the end, the meeting ends up being with the entire Sales & Marketing department and another couple of projects emerge from this.

Chastened, and a bit alarmed, the CEO has a similar conversation with the Product Development side of the house. One or two other so-called "internal projects" emerge. In addition, the CEO makes a few decisions about things that should also be on the list. They are:

- All of these projects should be being properly project managed. He's not sure whether they are or not, but he knows (from Chapter 6) that each of the projects is going to require an additional 10% of its total effort for project management. He wants to make sure that's factored in, so he's going to separate it out as a separate line item.

- He's also going to put in a line item called 'Product Support'. This is so that the three people who provide that will also be included in his calculations.

- Because the area of technology in which the company finds itself is so fast-changing, the CEO knows they will have to spend some of their time looking at new products and technologies. So he's going to have a line item called "New technologies".

- He's also going to include a line item called "Quality system". The company is installing a new quality system and he reckons that over the 18 month period that he's looking at some proportion of peoples' time is going to go into that. He needs to allow for it.

- Also, he's going to include a line item called "Training". In general, the people he has are very new/young/inexperienced. In addition, both the area of technology that the company is in and the development tools that the company uses are very new and fast-changing. Previously, working with the HR person, he has worked out that – to stay current and work effectively – his Product Development people need about 7 days training a year. That's going to come to 10 days over 18 months.

- Next, he is going to include a line item called "Contingency". Is it likely that nothing will change in this industry or in this company over the next 18 months? Come off it! Of course things will change. Of course unexpected things will occur. He needs to have something in reserve to cover those.

Moreover, he has to make some assumptions about the additional projects that they will have to do over the next 18 months. He makes a couple of assumptions:

- Sales have about a 50% hit rate. In other words, taking everything into account, they tend to win about half the business that they bid for. So, the CEO has another conversation with the Head of Sales & Marketing about what proposals they have out, or are likely to put out, over the next 18 months. He takes 50% of this and that gives him a couple more projects for his list.
- Finally, he gazes into his CEO's crystal ball and just tries to imagine what else could occur over the next 18 months that might cause more projects to go onto the list.

So, having done all this work, this is what his list ends up looking like (Figure 8.1).

Figure 8.1 Acme's initial project list

	THE ACME COMPANY - PROJECT LIST		
1	3041		
	3141		
2		For Sweden	
3		For France	
4		For Spain	
5	USB Widget		
	3141 New architecture		
6		Sweden	
7		France	
8		Spain	
	Standalone gizmo		
9		Sweden	
10		France	
11		Spain	
	System-wide device		
12		Sweden	
13		France	
14		Spain	
	NPK 1622		
15		France	
16		Sweden	
17		Spain	
18	Divergent NPK		
	CEF		
19		Variant 1	
20		Varian 2	
	Product Support		
21			Existing products
22			New products
23	Other Variants		
24	New technologies		
25	Quality system		
26	Training		
27	Contingency		
28	Project management		

(3) Figure out the status of each project

The CEO then assesses the status of each project. He does this not by reading it from the status report but rather by going and asking each project manager. He asks them the three questions given earlier in the chapter and marks the projects accordingly. What he finds is summarised in figure 8.2.

Figure 8.2 Acme's initial project status

	THE ACME COMPANY - PROJECT LIST			STATUS	Red / Amber / Green / Blue
1	3041			On target	5
	3141				
2		For Sweden		No written plan	0
3		For France		Some problems	3
4		For Spain		On target	5
5	USB Widget			On target	5
	3141 New architecture				
6		Sweden		On target	5
7		France		On target	5
8		Spain		On target	5
	Standalone gizmo				
9		Sweden		On target	5
10		France		On target	5
11		Spain		On target	5
	System-wide device				
12		Sweden		Out of control	-1
13		France		Out of control	-1
14		Spain		Some problems	3
	NPK 1622				
15		France		Out of control	-1
16		Sweden		On target	5
17		Spain		Some problems	3
18	Divergent NPK			On target	5
	CEF				
19		Variant 1		Out of control	-1
20		Varian 2		On target	5
21	Other Variants			Some problems	3
	Product Support				
22		Existing products		Some problems	3
23		New products		Spme problems	3
24	New technologies			No written plan	0
25	Quality system			On target	5
26	Training			On target	5
27	Contingency			Out of control	-1
28	Project management			Out of control	-1
				Total of scores	82.00
				OPI	2.93
	Green (5) = On Track:			14	
	Amber (3) = Warning! Some Problems:			6	
	Blue (0) = No Plan Exists:			2	
	Red (-1) = Runaway Project:			6	
	Status unknown				
	TOTAL NUMBER OF PROJECTS			28	
	TOTAL AT RISK (Red or Blue)			8	

For the regular projects – numbers 1-21 – the CEO gets the status exactly as described above. For the others he has to interpret the guidelines a bit and this is how he chooses to do that:

- The Product Support people report – as they always do – that they have too few many people for all of the support calls and other work they have to do. The CEO chooses to rate this Amber on the basis that he wants to check at some stage the supply demand situation here which, he believes, nobody has ever done before.
- "New technologies" definitely has no written plan. In fact getting to work on new technologies is generally regarded as the plum assignment in Acme. "Techies" get to work on cool stuff and there are no deadlines. The only problem tends to be that people are continuously pulled out of working on new technologies to go and fill gaps on other projects.
- The quality system has a plan that the very meticulous HR Manager (who is a former techie and is double-jobbing running the quality system) put together.
- Training – yes, there is a training plan courtesy of the selfsame, previously mentioned HR Manager.
- There is no contingency (as in spare capacity) currently – at least as not as far as the CEO is aware – and he would be surprised if project management has been factored into any plan. He therefore declares both of these to be Red (Out of control).

(4) Calculate the Organisational Performance Indicator (OPI)

Acme's OPI is 2.9 – partway between -1 (the worst) and 5 (the best). At least 8 projects are at risk. It's food for thought for the CEO as he turns the page and discovers what he must do next.

Scaling up/scaling down

I think it's pretty clear that scaling down this example to a smaller organisation simply means that you would end with a smaller list. As for scaling up for a larger organisation, the best way to do that would be to sub-divide it by, say, department or group and then let each one of those do what was described above.

At-a-glance summary

1. Decide what period of time you want to look at.
2. Make a list of all the projects you are doing or plan to do over that period.
3. Figure out the status of each project.
4. Calculate the Organisational Performance Indicator (OPI).

Chapter 9

Step 2: Estimate The Demand

It should really come as no surprise that the next couple of steps in installing a Zero Waste system involve looking at supply and demand. Let's start with the demand.

Now that you've got your list of projects, you've got to figure out the demand of these projects, i.e. how much work is required to complete each of them. Really, there is only one way to do this accurately. That is to estimate each of the projects as described in Chapter 5.

But that could take a lot of time and my sense is that, if that was what I now asked you to do, that would be the end of this journey. You'd say "thanks but no thanks", close the book and that'd be it.

Happily, there are three other ways you could go about estimating the projects. While none of these are as accurate as the way in Chapter 5 and while all projects will eventually have to be estimated properly, the three alternative ways described here have the advantage that they are quick to do. So here they are – your four possibilities for estimating the demand of each of these projects:

1. Estimate the projects as described in Chapter 5.
2. Estimate the projects based on their life cycle.
3. Use the how many people/how long/full-time or not method.
4. Estimate the projects using Small/Medium/Large.

They're described in turn.

(1) Estimate the projects as described in Chapter 5

Estimate each of the projects using the estimating method described in Chapter 5.

(2) Estimate the projects based on their life cycle

Sometimes, projects consist of a standard set of phases that they go through. Many product development projects, for example, go through phases like:

1. Figure out the requirements that the product must satisfy
2. Design it
3. Build it
4. Test it.

Furthermore, the ratio of these phases to each other (i.e. the amount of work involved in each phase compared to the others) tends to be (or should be, if the project is run properly) pretty much the same. So, for example, for the phases above the ratio might be something like this:

Phase	Ratio of work
1. Figure out the requirements that the product must satisfy	1
2. Design it	3
3. Build it	8
4. Test it	4

So if your projects are like this, then this method will work for you provided you know the ratios. How can you know or find out the ratios? Well, just look at some project that was completed successfully (assuming there is such a thing!) and get the ratios from that. If you're lucky you'll have records (timesheets, for example) of how much work went into each phase. If you're not so lucky, you'll just have to work it out as follows.

Get with some people who worked on or who know about this

project. Try to get them to recall how much work went into each phase. They can do this quite simply by trying to remember:

- how many people worked in each phase;
- for how long; and
- whether these people were full-time or not.

So the conversation might go something like this. "In the requirements phase, Charlie, Bert and Pete worked on it. Charlie was full-time, the other two probably two days a week. It lasted a month". So the total work in this phase then was:

- Charlie – 1 person for 1 month full-time = 1 man-month; Bert and Pete – 2 people for 1 month, 4 days a week between them = 2 man-months x 4/5 = 8/5 = 1.6 man-months. So the total here would be 2.6 man-months.

You would do this for the remaining phases and then extract the ratio. Having done this you then estimate the first phase of each project (using the how many people/how long/full-time or not method) and apply the ratio to get the other phases.

(3) Use the how many people/how long/full-time or not method

When there is no common life cycle amongst the projects – or for projects which don't fit into the life cycle – you can use the same:

- how many people worked in each phase;
- for how long; and
- whether these people were full-time or not method to do the estimation.
  It'll just take you a bit longer.

(4) Estimate the projects using Small/Medium/Large

One final way to come at this problem – it has the advantage of being the quickest, the disadvantage of being the least accurate – is to classify the projects into Small/Medium/Large. People often think in these terms. You often hear people say things like "Oh that's a small project" or "that's going to be a huge project."

OK, so if you think one of the projects is Small, try to quantify it using the:

- how many people are working on it;
- for how long; and
- whether these people are full-time or not method.

This will give you a number of man-months. You can now look at the rest of your list of projects and see if any of the others are roughly of the same size. These are the Small projects.

Now, look at the remaining list. Are all these projects the same size? If yes, try and quantify one of these using the how many people/how long/full-time or not method. Then all these remaining projects are your Mediums.

If the remaining projects are *not* all the same, then try to classify them into Medium and Large. You can have an Extra Large category if you need it. Then quantify one of each using the how many people/how long/full-time or not method. Then you can estimate the remaining projects by fitting them into one or other of these categories.

However you end up doing it, you will now have estimated all of your projects. Now just add all these up to give the overall total. This is the demand (work to be done) for your organisation.

Worked Example – Step 2: Measure The Demand

The CEO gets some people together to work out the demand. He gets the Head of Product Development and the three Team/Section Leaders. They agree pretty quickly that all of their development projects follow a standard life cycle consisting of four phases. These are:

1. Specification
2. Engineering Development
3. Field Trial
4. Production

This will take care of the bulk of the projects. (We'll see how they deal with the other ones below.)

They analyse a successful project using the how many people/how long/full-time or not method and establish that their ratio is:

Phase	Ratio of work
1. Specification	1
2. Engineering Development	8
3. Field Trial	1
4. Production.	1

They use this as a guideline but, as they go through the projects, they are prepared to modify it for specific circumstances on specific projects.

Since Product Support doesn't follow the standard life cycle, the way they estimate this is as follows: they simply ask how many people they will need over the period they're looking at – remember it's 18 months – to support existing and new products. The answer they come up with is two people for existing products and three people for new products. This then converts into an estimate of 78 weeks (one and a half years at 52 weeks per year) x the number of people.

New technologies are estimated in exactly the same way. They assume an average of two people in new technologies for the duration. For the quality system they do it like this – there are currently 26 people working on the projects spread between product development (23) and Product Support (3). They plan to hire in additional 6 people starting January 1 of the following year. This will be a total of 32 people. They assume that each of the 32 people involved in the projects will have to spend 4 days over the 18 months working on the quality system. This gives a figure of 128 person-days and they round this up to 26 person-weeks. For training they do something similar. They assume 32 people x 2 weeks training per person giving 64 person-weeks.

Contingency is calculated at 15% of the total work in the projects and project management at 10% of the total work in the projects. The results of their work are shown in Figure 9.1. The total demand is 5,550 man-weeks.

Figure 9.1 Acme – Demand

	THE ACME COMPANY - PROJECT LIST			Work (in MW)
1	**3041**	To finish it		8
	3141			
2		For Sweden		305
3		For France		172
4		For Spain		64
5	**USB Widget**			48
	3141 New architecture			
6		Sweden		312
7		France		64
8		Spain		64
	Standalone gizmo			
9		Sweden		232
10		France		68
11		Spain		68
	System-wide device			
12		Sweden		95
13		France		20
14		Spain		20
	NPK 1622			
15		France		720
16		Sweden		128
17		Spain		128
18	**Divergent NPK**			1032
	CEF			
19		Variant 1		128
20		Varian 2		128
21	**Other Variants**			0
	Product Support			
22		Existing products		156
23		New products		234
24	**New technologies**			156
25	**Quality system**			26
26	**Training**			64
27	**Contingency @**		15%	666
28	**Project management**		10%	444
				5550

Scaling up/scaling down
Your list will just be longer or shorter, depending on how many projects you have.

At-a-glance summary

1. Estimate each of your projects using any of the four methods:

- Estimate the projects as described in Chapter 5.
- Estimate the projects based on their life cycle.
- Use the how many people/how long/full-time or not method.
- Estimate the projects using Small/Medium/Large.

2. Add up the individual estimates to give the demand.

Chapter 10

Step 3: Measure The Supply

Now that you've measured the demand, you've got to measure the supply. Here's how to do that:

1.   Figure out how many people you have available for projects.
2.   For each person, work out how much time they can make available. Get people to do a Dance Card, as described in Chapter 5, if you (or they) are in any doubt about their availability.
3.   If you plan to hire any people in the period that you're looking at, repeat 1 and 2 for them.
4.   Add all of these numbers up to give the total.
5.   Calculate the Supply Demand Ratio (SDR).

Calculating the Supply – Demand Ratio (SDR)
The OPI was a snapshot of your organisation – an assessment at a point in time. There is something else you need as well. You need to get a sense of how things might evolve in the future. If your snapshot looks good, will it continue to do so? And if it looks bad, but you feel you can make it better, how likely is that? To answer these and similar questions, you need to look at your organisation's Supply-Demand Ratio (SDR).

The SDR of an organisation compares the number of people available to work on projects (supply) with the amount of work to be done on projects (demand). Obviously, given what we said earlier, the supply – demand ration should always be 1. In other words, there should be enough people to do all the work or else the work won't get done. (In my experience, it is rarely if ever 1 – but let's leave that for now.)

The SDR is simply demand divided by supply. I hope you can see the significance of the SDR. If the SDR is less than 1, it means there are more than enough people to do all the work. If the SDR is equal to 1 there are just enough people to do all the work. If the SDR is greater than 1 then you're in trouble. It means that even if the OPI showed that all of the projects were Green/on target, the fact that the SDR is greater than 1 means that these projects will *inevitably* start to drift off target. Let me be absolutely clear what I mean by this. It is not that this drifting off target *might* happen or *sometimes* happens. It is *guaranteed to happen* because of the discrepancy between the supply and the demand.

Worked Example – Step 3 Measure The Supply

The CEO meets with the HR person, the Head of Product Development and the three Team/Section Leaders. They are able to work out the following pretty quickly.

Currently there are 26 people available full-time to work on projects. If we take out 4 weeks holiday, 2 weeks public holidays and assume no sickness, then each of these 26 people can contribute 46 weeks work in a year. So over one and half years, these people will contribute 26 x 46 x 1.5 = 1,794 person-weeks. The 6 new hires are due to start on 1 January so they will contribute 6 x 46 = 276 person-weeks. This gives a total of 2,070 person-weeks.

The SDR = Demand/Supply = 5,550/2,070 = 2.7.

Bad news. In this organisation, there is 2.7 times more work to be done than there is time and people available to do it.

Scaling up/scaling down
For a larger number of people in your organisation it will just take you a little bit longer to do the calculations.

At-a-glance summary
1. Figure out how many people you have available for projects.
2. For each person, work out how much time they can make available.
    Get people to do a Dance Card, as described in Chapter 5, if you (or

they) are in any doubt about their availability.
3. If you plan to hire any people in the period that you're looking at, repeat 1 and 2 for them.
4. Add all of these numbers up to give the total.
5. Calculate the Supply Demand Ratio (SDR).

Chapter 11

Step 4: Prioritise The Projects

First, an important point. It's another one of those pay-attention-closely moments. I fully accept that there are issues other than having the right amount of people involved in getting projects done. One of key ones is the whole question of skills/knowledge/experience. People are not interchangeable. Different people have different skills/knowledge/experience and the set of skills/knowledge/experience required to do one project is not, in general, the same as that required to do another.

But any talk of skills/knowledge/experience becomes irrelevant if supply and demand are not the same. Only when that problem has been resolved can you start to consider the question of skills/knowledge/experience.

If your supply (from Chapter 10) turns to be less than or equal to your demand (from Chapter 9), then you're OK – for now! But what if new projects come along to change that? And if your supply is less than your demand then you've got a real problem. This means that all of the projects are not going to get done. I'll say that again but louder so that you hear it, don't forget it and understand the full significance of it: THIS MEANS THAT ALL OF THE PROJECTS ARE NOT GOING TO GET DONE. And no amount of wishing it were otherwise, pretending that's not what's going to happen, JFDI, sweating your resources or anything else is going to make it otherwise.

So now you have a choice. You can decide straight up, right now, which projects are going to get done. Or you can just ignore this uncomfortable fact, go into some kind of denial and let it all roll anyway. Wagons ho! Start projects, make commitments to stakeholders, assign people, start burning budgets – and see what happens. You're not going to decide which projects are going to get done. You're going to let fate or luck take that decision.

Sounds like a good idea? No, I didn't think so. But if you think it is, then once again close the book and pass it on to somebody whom you think needs it.

If you think having fate/luck run your business is *not* a good idea, then it means that you're going to decide which projects are not going to be done. In order to do that, you're going to have to prioritise your projects in some way. Here's how to do that. There are basically two ways:

1.   If I could only do one thing what would it be?
2.   Identify the factors which make up the prioritisation decision.

(1) If I could only do one thing what would it be?

This is as simple as it sounds. You take your list of projects and ask the question, "if I could only do one project, which one would it be?" This becomes your #1 priority. You then take the remaining list and ask the question again. If I could only do one project which one would it be? This is your #2 priority. You keep on doing this until the list is prioritised. You can't have a joint priority – a sort of 7(a) and 7(b) – each item is either more important or less important than each other item.

(2) Identify the factors which make up the prioritisation decision

So what might these factors be? Well, they can be almost anything. Examples would be things like:

- Gross profit or savings that the project is going to generate.
- Who the customer is.
- The project produces something that is necessary for longer-term growth/survival.
- And so on.

If you're going to use this method, then best way to do it is like this:

1.   Identify the factors that you think are relevant.
2.   Decide which is the most important, then the next most important, then the next most important and so on. So, just to take a simple example, you might decide that the identity of the customer is the most important parameter. In other words, you're saying that projects for certain customers will always take priority over those of others. Then within that, you might decide that gross profit was the most important parameter. So you would prioritise your projects thus then:

1.   Customer A Project 1 (Profit = 100,000 euros)
2.   Customer A Project 2 (Profit = 60,000)
3.   Customer A Project 3 (Profit = 50,000)
4.   Customer B Project 1 (Profit = 75,000)
5.   Customer B Project 2 (Profit = 60,000)
6.   Customer C project 1 (Profit = 70,000)
7.   And so on.

It may take you a few reiterations before you get this right. You may do it the first time, look at the result and decide you're not really happy with that. OK, so put in some additional factor(s) that make(s) it more like the way you think it should be. Eventually, after a handful of reiterations, your prioritisation algorithm should settle down.

Worked Example – Step 4: Prioritise the Projects

The CEO gets with the Head of Product Development and the Head of Sales & Marketing. They eventually prioritise the projects as shown in Figure 11.1. These are some of the issues they run into and this is how they choose to solve them:

•   They are surprised when "Product Support – Existing products" comes in at #1. However, how could it be otherwise? They have to support what is already out in the field. And they get a slice of revenue from this anyway.

- There is a lot of argument before "Quality System" and "Project Management" get #2 and #3 respectively. The CEO eventually swings it by saying that if "we're not doing what we're doing right, then there's no point in being in business". Surely that applies to "Training" too, the Head of Product Development counters. But the CEO rejects this. There is a lot of stuff they can do with their current staff and current level of training.

Figure 11.1 Acme's prioritised project list

PRIORITY	THE ACME COMPANY - PROJECT LIST			Work (in MW
1	Product Support - Existing products			156
2	Quality system			26
3	Project management		10%	444
4	Divergent NPK			1032
5	3141	For Sweden		305
6	3141 New architecture	Sweden		312
7	Standalone gizmo	Sweden		232
8	3141	For France		172
9	NPK 1622	Sweden		128
10	NPK 1622	Spain		128
11	CEF	Variant 1		128
12	CEF	Varian 2		128
13	3041	To finish it		8
14	3141	For Spain		64
15	USB Widget			48
16	NPK 1622	France		720
17	System-wide device	Spain		20
18	3141 New architecture	France		64
19	3141 New architecture	Spain		64
20	System-wide device	France		20
21	System-wide device	Sweden		95
22	Standalone gizmo	France		68
23	Standalone gizmo	Spain		68
24	Product Support - New products			234
25	New technologies			156
26	Training			64
27	Contingency @		15%	666
28	Other Variants			0
				5550

Scaling up/scaling down
Your list will just be longer or shorter, depending on how many projects you have.

At-a-glance summary
Prioritise your projects using:

1.   If I could only do one thing what would it be; or
2.   Identify the factors which make up the prioritisation decision.

Chapter 12

Step 5: Make The Cut

If your supply is greater than or equal to your demand, then you can probably skip this chapter. Otherwise, read on.

For you this is now the most difficult bit. Given that your demand is greater than your supply, you now have to decide what's going to get done and what's not going to get done. Essentially, you have four choices – What, When, Work, Quality. Here they are in turn:

1. **What.** Don't do some things at all. The prioritisation you did in Chapter 11 will enable you to determine which things.
2. **When.** Don't do some things in the period of time that you're looking at, i.e. move them off into the future.
3. **Work.** Get more people. There are three aspect to this:

   1. You could add more people. (But don't forget what we've said previously about adding people to projects.)
   2. You might be able to outsource or sub-contract some projects. This will obviously add costs because you will have to pay for the subcontracting. Remember too that it won't reduce the work involved in the projects to zero because you will still have to manage the subcontracts.
   3. I know. I know. You're saying what about the third option? The obvious, traditional third option – when am

I going to talk about that? It's the option encapsulated in that glorious question, "Are these plans based on a five day week?" The third option, you're saying, is that you could "sweat your resources". OK – this is where you're going to have to let this one go. It's not an option, as discussed in Chapter 2. You try to do this and *you will drive productivity down*. So let it go. Now and for all time. It may have been what you've done in the past but it's not what you're going to do in the future. Wave it goodbye. Wish it well and say ,"That's it – I'm not gonna do that any more."

4. **Quality.** There are two aspects to this:

    1. Tinker with the quality of what you're doing. The most obvious approach is to cut out or shorten testing or other quality assurance type activities. Not a good idea, I think you'll agree.
    2. Find better ways to do things – better tools, methods, procedures.

You are going to find this step to be the most difficult thing you have done so far. Indeed, as the head of an organisation that has to deliver to its customers, it's going to be one of the hardest things you will ever do.

But from your point of view, it means you take back the running of your organisation from fate/luck. From your customers' point of view there's a benefit too. They know where they stand. Customers aren't entitled to expect miracles. If they do, it's only because you've given them miracles in the past. But if you continue to deliver miracles then, sooner or later, it will all come horribly unstuck as you run into the unforgiving nature of supply and demand.

So give up miracles and let your customer know how (s)he stands. It's the recipe for a long and happy future for all concerned.

Worked Example – Step 4 Prioritise the Projects

The CEO gets with the Head of Product Development and the Head of

Sales & Marketing. They look at their choices from the list above and come to the conclusion that, in reality, they have the following choices:

- They decide that, for them, not doing things at all and not doing things in the next 18 months amount to the same thing. With such a huge gap between supply and demand, not doing certain things is definitely going to have to be part of their approach.
- They can't hire any more full-time people – the budget won't allow it.
- They can subcontract certain small projects.
- They are not (any longer) going to sweat their resources. The whole idea of this Zero Waste effort has been to find a better way. If this really is a better way, then, by definition, they're going to have to resist the temptation to do this.
- They won't tinker with quality.
- If they can find better ways to do things, they will.

Having made these decisions, they now look at their prioritised list again (in Figure 12.1 overleaf).

Figure 12.1 Acme – Prioritised list of projects showing cumulative work

PRIORITY	THE ACME COMPANY - PROJECT LIST			Work (in MW)	Cumulative Work (in MW)
1	Product Support - Existing products			156	156
2	Quality system			26	182
3	Project management		10%	444	626
4	Divergent NPK			1032	1658
5	3141	For Sweden		305	1963
6	3141 New architecture	Sweden		312	2275
7	Standalone gizmo	Sweden		232	2507
8	3141	For France		172	2679
9	NPK 1622	Sweden		128	2807
10	NPK 1622	Spain		128	2935
11	CEF	Variant 1		128	3063
12	CEF	Varian 2		128	3191
13	3041	To finish it		8	3199
14	3141	For Spain		64	3263
15	USB Widget			48	3311
16	NPK 1622	France		720	4031
17	System-wide device	Spain		20	4051
18	3141 New architecture	France		64	4115
19	3141 New architecture	Spain		64	4179
20	System-wide device	France		20	4199
21	System-wide device	Sweden		95	4294
22	Standalone gizmo	France		68	4362
23	Standalone gizmo	Spain		68	4430
24	Product Support - New products			234	4664
25	New technologies			156	4820
26	Training			64	4884
27	Contingency @		15%	666	5550
28	Other Variants			0	
			Demand =	5,550	
			Supply =	2,070	

1. They decide that they can subcontract the small project called "System-wide device" – all three variants, France, Sweden and Spain. Together, these projects come to 135 person-weeks. They replace this by a (guessed) figure of 4 person-weeks to organise and manage the subcontract. See Figure 12.2.

2. It is now clear that some projects are going to have to be dropped. That will reduce the amount of work that goes into "Product Support – new products". They decide they will have only two people here – the same as "Product Support – Existing products"

– rather then the three they had originally planned.

3.　　They realise – and this is a thing that often happens – it's not just a convenience for the author! – that the projects "3141" and "3141 new architecture" (both for Sweden) are essentially the same project. In other words, they have inadvertently double counted the work here. They replace it with one project with a slightly higher number of man-weeks. In terms of its status though, they note that they will have to write a new plan for this composite project. This gets them to Figure 12.2.

Figure 12.2 Acme – First attempt to match supply to demand

PRIORITY	THE ACME COMPANY - PROJECT LIST		Work (in MW)	Cumulative Work (in MW)	STATUS	Red / Amb Green / Bl.
1	Product Support - Existing products		156	156	Some problems	3
2	Quality system		26	182	On target	5
4	Divergent NPK		1032	1214	On target	5
5	3141 New architecture	For Sweden	330	1544	No written plan	0
7	Standalone gizmo	Sweden	232	1776	On target	5
8	3141	For France	172	1948	Some problems	3
9	NPK 1622	Sweden	128	2076	On target	5
10	NPK 1622	Spain	128	2204	Some problems	3
11	CEF	Variant 1	128	2332	Out of control	-1
12	CEF	Varian 2	128	2460	On target	5
13	3041	To finish it	8	2468	On target	5
14	3141	For Spain	64	2532	On target	5
15	USB Widget		48	2580	On target	5
16	NPK 1622	France	720	3300	Out of control	-1
17	System-wide devices (3)	Spain	4	3304	Some problems	3
18	3141 New architecture	France	64	3368	On target	5
19	3141 New architecture	Spain	64	3432	On target	5
22	Standalone gizmo	France	68	3500	On target	5
23	Standalone gizmo	Spain	68	3568	On target	5
24	Product Support - New products		156	3724	Spme problems	3
25	New technologies		156	3880	No written plan	0
26	Training		64	3944	On target	5
		SUBTOTAL	3944			
27	Contingency @	15%	592		Out of control	-1
3	Project management	10%	394		Out of control	-1
		Demand =	4,930			
		Supply =	2,070			

It's still not enough so they have to keep going.

4.　　Training gets cut completely. The CEO explains the rationale for this. He says that it appears now that, for the next 18 months, Acme is going to have to focus on just delivering its current commitments. There will be little or *no* work on 'New technologies". As he says these words he realises the full implications of this statement. Realistically, there is going to be no work on the job "New technologies" and there will be even less on "Product Support – New products" so that the figure which they revised only a few minutes ago gets cut further. (They cut it to one person.)

5. They are unable to resist the urge to cut contingency to 10%. Their argument is that if the Zero Waste approach is worth its salt, they should need less contingency for unexpected events and fire fights.

6. With pain in their hearts, they cut the bottom four (in terms of priority) projects. They are not going to do them. The Head of Sales & Marketing is going to have to square this with any customers. Oooh – that's gonna hurt! They're at Figure 12.3.

Figure 12.3 Acme – Second pass to match supply to demand

PRIORITY	THE ACME COMPANY - PROJECT LIST		Work (in MW)	Cumulative Work (in MW)	STATUS
1	Product Support - Existing products		156	156	Some problems
2	Quality system		26	182	On target
3	Divergent NPK		1032	1214	On target
4	3141 New architecture	For Sweden	330	1544	No written plan
5	Standalone gizmo	Sweden	232	1776	On target
6	3141	For France	172	1948	Some problems
7	NPK 1622	Sweden	128	2076	On target
8	NPK 1622	Spain	128	2204	Some problems
9	CEF	Variant 1	128	2332	Out of control
10	CEF	Varian 2	128	2460	On target
11	3041	To finish it	8	2468	On target
12	3141	For Spain	64	2532	On target
13	USB Widget		48	2580	On target
14	NPK 1622	France	720	3300	Out of control
15	System-wide devices (3)	Spain	4	3304	Some problems
16	3141 New architecture	France	0	3304	On target
17	3141 New architecture	Spain	0	3304	On target
18	Standalone gizmo	France	0	3304	On target
19	Standalone gizmo	Spain	0	3304	On target
20	Product Support - New products		78	3382	Spme problems
21	New technologies		0	3382	No written plan
22	Training		0	3382	On target
		SUBTOTAL	3382		
	Contingency @	10%	338		Out of control
	Project management	10%	338		Out of control
		Demand =	4,058		
		Supply =	2,070		

But it still isn't enough. They need a big hit to make the numbers work.

7.   With even greater pain in their hearts, they pull the plug on 'NPK 1622'. That's really going to hurt them with those customers.

And they're still not there. Finally, the Head of Sales & Marketing's nerve breaks. He throws a "freaker" about how difficult it was to land these customers in the first place and now look at what he's going to have to do – go back and tell them that their projects aren't going to happen. These are only estimates – and maybe not very accurate estimates at that. What if these numbers *are* wrong?

The CEO has some sympathy for his position and this issue of the accuracy of the estimates is worrying him too. What if they are wrong? He realises that they won't have better estimates until they have done proper plans for all of the projects and estimated them as described in Chapter 5. So, maybe, he tells the Head of Sales & Marketing, that they can put off doing anything with customers until that's been done.

This calms the Head of Sales & Marketing a bit who had had visions of having to be on planes and having very difficult conversations with customers in the next few days. "So, let's estimate and plan these projects properly as a matter of urgency" says the CEO. "And also," he continues, "let's make a working assumption for the moment that they are correct. Given that it doesn't look like we can cut any more projects," – the Head of Sales & Marketing emits a loud sigh of relief – "let's plan to hire three contract people to try to make up the gap. If we can get them in straight away, we'll get 3 times 78 weeks from them. That's 234 man-weeks".

Finally, the CEO has one more bright idea. If they're going to be running these projects properly, and if the new quality system is in place, then maybe the incremental increase in product support will be small because the new products will be developed to such a high level of quality. The temptation is too much and they cut "Product Support – new products" completely.

They call it a day at Figure 12.4, overleaf.

Figure 12.4 Acme – Third and final pass to match supply to demand

PRIORITY	THE ACME COMPANY - PROJECT LIST		Work (in MW)	Cumulative Work (in MW)	STATUS
1	Product Support - Existing products		156	156	Some problems
2	Quality system		26	182	On target
3	Divergent NPK		1032	1214	On target
4	3141 New architecture	For Sweden	330	1544	No written plan
5	Standalone gizmo	Sweden	232	1776	On target
6	3141	For France	172	1948	Some problems
7	NPK 1622	Sweden	128	2076	On target
8	NPK 1622	Spain	128	2204	Some problems
9	CEF	Variant 1	128	2332	Out of control
10	CEF	Varian 2	128	2460	On target
11	3041	To finish it	8	2468	On target
12	3141	For Spain	64	2532	On target
13	USB Widget		48	2580	On target
14	NPK 1622	France	0	2580	Out of control
15	System-wide devices (3)	Spain	4	2584	Some problems
16	Product Support - New products		0	2584	Spme problems
		SUBTOTAL	2584		
	Contingency @	10%	258		Out of control
	Project management	10%	258		Out of control
		Demand =	3,101		
		Supply =	2,304		

The CEO summarises what this final picture says. They are definitely going to do projects 1-8. The workload here is 2,204 man-weeks. Adding 10% contingency and 10% for project management gives 2,644 man-weeks, but the CEO declares this "close enough for government work". They will revisit this when the projects have been estimated accurately.

Projects 9-13 will have to wait pending the estimation of projects 1-8. Then they will see what they will see, the CEO says. At the moment it looks like everything else isn't going to happen, but he's going to wait until projects 1-8 have been estimated to get a sense of the overall accuracy of this exercise.

It's as much as they can do right now. They agree to reconvene the meeting in two week's time. In the intervening period, projects 1-8 will have to be estimated accurately.

Footnote

It may seem like I have engineered the figures at the Acme Company to provide a particularly dramatic case study. In fact, I didn't. These figures are based on, and not a million miles away from, a real-life situation that I encountered. While it was a severe case of supply demand imbalance, I'd have to say it wasn't uncommon.

Scaling up/scaling down

You'll have more or less work to do depending on how long your project list is and how severe your supply demand imbalance is. What there is no doubt about is that you'll – potentially – have very difficult decisions to make.

At-a-glance summary

Match supply to demand by doing some combination of the following:

1. **What.** Not doing some things at all.
2. **When.** Not doing some things in the period that you're looking at.
3. **Work.** Either actually adding more people or sub-contracting things.
4. **Quality.** Finding better ways to do things.

PART THREE
Chapter 13

What You've Achieved

You now have all the elements of your Zero Waste system in place. You're ready to run your system.

But before you do that it's worth looking at what you have achieved in terms of the sources of big waste that we spoke about in Chapter 2. If you remember, there were seven of them. Let's look at them in turn.

1. There is waste every time you switch people between projects

Things change. And so you will never eliminate this source of waste completely. But I hope you can see that you have drastically reduced it. Because there are now enough people to do all the work, there will be far less occurrences of having to switch resources to deal with fire fights on particular projects.

You may argue that all you have done is to cut a whole bunch of projects out of the projects list so that there are enough people to do all of the work. My first answer to that will be, "Yes, and your problem with that is what exactly?"

But my second answer will be that if you hadn't cut the projects from the list, fate/luck would have cut them. Certain projects were always going to not get done (because there weren't enough people to do them). Now, at least, you have had a chance to make a conscious choice about this versus just letting it unfold and seeing what would happen.

In the new scheme of things the projects that won't get done are the ones that you have identified as being least important to the organisation. As things stood originally, you wouldn't have known which projects were going to get done. (Note that you also wouldn't have known which projects mattered most to the organisation). Worse than that, you wouldn't have known, right up to the end, exactly which ones were going to make it.

2. There is waste every time you don't plan a project properly

You have not dealt with this yet. That is where you will be turning your attention next (in Chapter 14).

3. There is waste every time you have to deal with a fire fight

With less projects and enough people to do all the work, there will be less fire fights. Planning the projects will reduce the number of fire fights much further.

4. There is waste because people are working long hours

There will be far less need for people to work long hours with the associated loss in productivity. Planning will improve this even further.

5. There is waste every time a project goes astray or is cancelled.

Because all of the projects are adequately resourced, there will be far less projects going astray or getting cancelled. There still needs to be good planning to make sure that this promise isn't dashed.

6. There is waste because morale goes down

Because there should be no more "death march" type projects with all the attendant suffering, morale should go up. Planning will secure this even further.

7. There is waste due to multitasking

Because supply and demand match, the need for multitasking is going to go down. However, we will return to this issue in Part 3.
 So we can summarise your achievements so far like this:

Cause of Waste	Dealt with in Part 2
1. Switching people between projects	Yes
2. Not planning projects properly	No
3. Having to deal with fire fights	Partly
4. Working long hours	Partly
5. Projects going astray or being cancelled	Partly
6. Morale going down	Partly
7. Multitasking	Partly

Chapter 14

Step 6: Plan Your Projects

You have your Zero Waste system in place. Now you're going to start running it.

You may remember, back in Chapter 8, that you did a "soft audit" of the projects, i.e. you asked the project manager what the status of the project was and, whatever they said, you took as being true. In general, when you do this you come up with projects in a variety of states. Some are on target; some have drifted a bit; some don't have a plan. If the project manager is very honest with themselves, they'll admit when a project has gone out of control. So even without going any further, after a soft audit, you know that some projects need to have their planning looked at or, indeed, to be replanned.

But, as mentioned already, the picture the soft audit gives is rarely the true one. Things are generally worse. And now is the time to look at all of that. You're going to do two things here:

1. For each project, *starting with the highest priority one and working your way down*:

    1.1 Figure out the true state of the project.
    1.2 Make sure that it has a good plan.
    1.3 Staff the project with as little multitasking as possible.

2. Deal with new projects.

1.1 Figure out the true state of the project

The following tests will tell you the correct status of a project:

- No work calculated in the plan.
- Supply and demand not the same.
- Do a PSI.

No work calculated in the plan

If the project plan contains no calculation of the work to be done – if, for example, it contains only a Gantt Chart showing duration and not work – then the plan is a turkey. There has been no attempt to calculate demand. Thus there is no understanding of how big the project is. However the project manager classified this project, you have to classify it as a Blue (No written plan).

Supply and Demand not the same

Somewhat similar to the previous case, if the demand has been calculated but the project manager cannot show you that there is adequate supply, then you'd have to classify this as a Red (Out of control).

Do a PSI

Do a PSI on the project as described in Chapter 6. (You could do one, the project manager could do one independently and you could compare scores.) If the project is fairly early in its life and the PSI is less than 40, then put the actions in train to get the PSI score up. (The low individual scores will point you at what you have to do.) Until then, you'd have to classify this project as Amber (Some problems).

If the project has been running for a while – if, for example, it was supposedly past its half-way mark – and the PSI was under 40, then you'd have to classify this project as a Red (Out of control).

Update your project list with these true scores.

1.2 Make sure that the project has a good plan

Now, depending on the project's status, do the following:

Red project (Out of control)

If a project is out of control, you need to understand why. Calculating a PSI will point you at the causes. As a cross check, you could look at the checklist below and see if any of the following apply to the project.

Twelve most common reasons why projects fail:

1. The goal of the project isn't defined properly.
2. The goal of the project is defined properly, but then changes to it aren't controlled.
3. Not all of the project stakeholders are identified.
4. Stakeholders are identified but win conditions aren't.
5. The project isn't planned/estimated properly.
6. The project isn't led properly.
7. The project is planned/estimated properly but then it isn't resourced as was planned.
8. The project is planned so that it has no contingency.
9. The expectations of project participants aren't managed.
10. The project is planned properly, but then progress against the plan is not monitored and controlled properly.
11. Project reporting is inadequate or non-existent.
12. When projects get into trouble, people believe the problem can be solved by some simple action, e.g. work harder, extend the deadline, add more resources.

For these out of control projects you need to:

a) Build a new plan as described in Chapter 6.
b) Include in this new plan fixes to any of the issues you've identified as being the cause of the project going off the rails.

This will return the status of the project to Green.

Blue project (No written plan)

You need to write one as described in Chapter 6, estimating the project properly. This will return the status of the project to Green.

Amber project (Some problems)
Fix whatever is causing the problems in order to return the project status to Green.

Green project (On target)
Just keep 'em that way!

1.3 Staff the project

(Remember as you read this that you're starting with the highest priority project and working your way down the list.) Now staff the project fully i.e. match supply to demand; make sure every job has somebody to do it.

But also do this *with the least amount of multitasking*. In other words, try to ensure that, as far as is humanly possible, everybody working on the project is working on it full-time. This will:

a) avoid delays caused by people having to go off and work on other things; and
b) reduce massively the lengthening effect we saw in Chapters 2 and 3 in the sections on multitasking.

Try to do everything you can to avoid having people multitasking. If the same person is required on several different projects, don't split them up! Get them to finish one first and then go to work on the next one (in the priority list). And there may be other more creative things you can do. If the same person has to work on several different projects, can you hire somebody in with the same skill set so that you don't have to spread the person across projects? Or can you train somebody else to have the same skill set? Or can you outsource the particular thing?

Ultimately projects will get done quicker by getting one out of the way and then going on to the next one, rather than by trying to get several done at the same time via multitasking. (If you would like further corroboration of this, read [5]).

(4) Deal with new projects

Things change. New projects come along. Projects which were massively important become less important or irrelevant because of changes in the business climate. A new or different project suddenly becomes essential because of something one of our competitors has done. The CEO has a great idea which actually turns out to be a great idea.

In the old way of doing things when this happened, the new project was just started up and people were pinched from other projects to staff it. Or the one which was suddenly less important suddenly found itself stripped of most or all of its people.

That's not how it will work now.

When an idea for a new project is born it goes onto a list. So too do suggestions about de-prioritising or changing the priority of projects.

Periodically then – once a week, initially if you want to, but it will generally increase to once every two weeks or once a month – the people who decide on such things hold a meeting. At the meetings they:

- Consider each project on the list in turn .
- Prioritise it.
- Fit it into the project priority list.
- Make the cut based on this revised priority list, i.e. they drop those projects which can no longer be staffed and only include projects which can be.

At-a-glance summary

1. For each project, *starting with the highest priority one and working your way down*:

    1.1. Figure out the true state of the project.
    1.2. Make sure that it has a good plan.
    1.3. Staff the project with as little multitasking as possible.

2. Deal with new projects by revising the priority list and making the cut again.

Chapter 15

Step 7: Track And Report Your Projects

You want to do two things here:

1. Track the status of all of the organisation's projects;
2. Report the status.

In theory now, there's nothing for you to do except let the people running the projects track them and report the status; and then you'll just summarise all of that into an overall status report for your organisation. That's the way it should work.

In reality, I'd like to think nobody would be that naïve. There's a Dilbert cartoon – you may have seen it. In it, Dilbert and his colleagues are having a meeting. The boss says, "Let's go round the table and give an update on each of our projects". Dilbert says,"My project is a pathetic series of poorly-planned, near-random acts. My life is a tragedy of emotional desperation". The boss says that "It's more or less customary to say that things are going fine". Dilbert says "I think I need a hug."

What the boss says is so true – it *is* more or less customary to say that things are going fine. And this is what most of the status reporting that you see and hear does. Let's look at some of them – the verbal ones first.

You ask how's it going and you're told it's "fine", "great", "everything's on target", "everything's under control" or the terrifying "we're 90% done" – which generally means that 90% of the time has gone, not that 90% of the task has been done.

And then you get the written status reports that are full of things like "tasks completed last week", "tasks planned for next week", "percentage complete", "critical issues", and so on – often sound and fury signifying nothing.

The upshot of this is that if you want to be prudent and make sure things don't go awry, you're going to have to do some tracking yourself. Now, obviously, you can't just duplicate what the people running the projects are doing. There are at least two reasons why that would be a bad idea: (a) the waste in the duplication of effort; (b) the upset you're going to cause with project managers feeling that you don't trust them, are second guessing them, looking over their shoulder and so on.

So here's what you're going to do. Each of the projects has a project plan which consists of a number of big phases which in turn consist of the detailed tasks. The project managers track the tasks. What you're going to do is have a project plan consisting of all of the projects with each of the projects in turn consisting of its big phases. You'll track the big phases. The situation is like this:

The project manager's view	Your view
Project	Organisation
Big phases	Projects
Tasks	Big phases.

So what you'll do is extract the big phases from each of their project plans and then insert them into yours. There's an example of doing this in the "Worked example" section later in the Chapter.

1. Track the status of all of the organisation's projects

"Tracking the plan" means two things. It means: (a) ensuring that what the plan says should be happening is happening; and (b) that what happens on the projects is reflected in the plan. Here's what to do:

1. Look down from top to bottom the line that represents today on your plan and identify any phase of any project that requires

some action by you today. (Once you get into doing this, rather than just looking down the line that represents today, you can look at a band maybe one or two or more weeks ahead. This is really good because you're now starting to look ahead and anticipate things before they become problems). Some phases may be in the hands of people you know to be consistently reliable. Every time they run a project for you, they deliver on target. So for these phases, there's nothing for you to do. Leave them alone and let them get on with it. Going and checking on these people is just going to upset/annoy them and is a complete waste of your time anyway. This is not to say to ignore them completely but any interaction with these people is likely to be along the lines of "What are you doing for the weekend?" or "Did you see the match last night?"

2. For any phase that does require some action by you today, note on your to-do list what needs to be done. Here's a bit more guidance:

• Not everybody is the rock solid, dependable guy we just described. Some people tend to be a bit more hit and miss. Mostly they do OK, but from time to time there are problems – they drop the ball. So you want to check on these guys but not so much that it turns into micro-management. So here's how this might work. You go to them and ask how the particular phase of their project is going. You want to *see* two things. First you want to see – not just be told that there has been – progress. If, for example, the phase is due to last four weeks, process a hundred widgets and the phase is half-way through, then fifty or so of the widgets should have been processed. In addition, you want to get a sense of how they plan to spend the rest of the time. They should show you their plan, which shows (hopefully) how the rest of the phase is going to get completed on time. If you get both these things then you could consider easing off a little bit and not checking on them so often. If not, you might want to come along again the next day and do a further check. You might even want to suggest to them a target they really need to reach by the end of the next day, the end of the week or whatever. Yes, sure, you're starting to drift now into micro-management, but if they can't be brought to the point where they can do it for themselves, then somebody is going to have to do it. And, unfortunately, that somebody is you – being the head of the organisation.

- The project managers under your control may be depending on people who don't report directly to them to do pieces of their project. These might be people in other departments or other companies such as subcontractors. These project managers may feel that there's not a lot that they can do in these situations – all they can do is hand over the job and trust to luck. You need to point out to them that, in reality, there's lots they can do. Right back at the beginning of the project, they can get this other person to give them estimates for the tasks, not to have estimates foisted on them. And if they're known to be an incredibly busy or under-pressure sort of person (or maybe even if they're not), the project manager should feel free to query the estimate with them. Are they sure that they'll be able to do this? Can this commitment be depended on? Then, as the time approaches when the task must be done, the project manager sends them a reminder that it's looming, it's coming up soon. Then, perhaps the day before the thing is due to start, an email. Are we good to go? Anything they need? Any excuse to nudge them again. Will all of this guarantee that they come through? Of course not. But then the project manager can go back, reschedule the thing. They can also make it clear to the person involved how badly this has affected them. If it's serious enough the project manager can and should mention it in his status report. Then, if all that fails to get the task done, the project manager can escalate it to you.

- If your project manager is brand new to project management, then the situation calls for micromanagement. A hands-off approach here will just cause problems. Not only that, hands-off would mean that you were guilty of throwing the person into the deep end to see if they sank or floated. Not a good idea. So here we're talking handholding, nurturing, training courses, on the job training, shadowing them, keeping a close eye on them, correcting them when they go wrong, passing on the benefit for your knowledge – in the hope that, as quickly as possible, they become useful members of society and you don't have to do that anymore.

(But notice that if they don't – and you want your projects done properly – then you're just going to have to keep on at them).

- And what if, after all this, they're still not running the projects properly and you're continuing to have problems with them? Then can I suggest a four-step approach as follows:

- **Step 1.** The first thing to ask yourself is whether it is you – and not they – who are the problem. Was the project assignment clear and unambiguous? Did you make clear what you wanted? Were you available to answer questions or to clarify things? Did *you* give *them* the resources – people, equipment, materials, training, support or whatever – to get the project done? Did you give them an impossible mission? Because if you're guilty of any of these things, then it shouldn't really come as any great surprise if they failed. Try to be honest here. It's all too easy to see the other person as the problem. But maybe the problem actually starts with you. If, having done this, you find that you were at fault, then correct whatever you did and see what happens. Maybe the problem goes away.

- **Step 2.** If, however, the problem fails to go away or you weren't at fault in the first place, then you need to move to Step 2, which is where you come up with an improvement plan. An improvement plan is simply a list of actions that you, the company or the project manager is going to take, along with dates by which those things are going to happen. (And, just to be clear, you're not talking long deadlines here – you're looking at a handful of weeks.) While you or the company may do one or two things – 'organise training' or 'monitor more closely' – things like that – the bulk of the actions will be undertaken by the project manager. In other words, the onus is on them to do the improving. This may solve the problem. If not, you go to Step 3.

- **Step 3** involves what you can think of as an extreme improvement plan – again with short deadlines. Basically, Step 3 is an ultimatum and is pretty much all about the project manager – take these actions, improve these things or something very bad will happen. This may solve the problem. If not then go to Step 4.

- **Step 4** is where the very bad thing happens. It can range from – at one end of the spectrum – moving them off the project to – to the other end – firing, along with all of the possibilities in between. What you actually choose will probably end up being a function of: (a) the type of organisation you are in (public sector versus private sector, for example); (b) the culture of the organisation. Also, it will almost certainly involve the Human Resources department – as, indeed, will Step 3. Needless to say, all of the actions at each of the steps should be documented.

3. OK, back to the main flow. Now go do the things on your to-do list.
4. As phases are completed update your plan with what actually happened, i.e. the phase was meant to last from this date to this date; it actually lasted from this date to this date. The phase was meant to use up so-many man-days; it actually used up so-many man-days. The phase was meant to cost X; it actually cost Y.
5. Check to see whether the durations, man-days or budget of any phases have changed. If they haven't then the project is on target. If they have improved, say nothing. If they have "dis-improved" then this is a warning sign. A single dis-improvement by itself may not be a problem, since the slip could be corrected the next time you do your tracking. But if each time you track the project the *trend* is not in the right direction, then this is a sign that you're in trouble. One way or another, you need to communicate the resulting status to the stakeholders.

(2) Report the status

Now that you know (from the tracking you've done) the status of all of the projects, you've got to communicate this to your stakeholders via a status report. I give a sample of the kind of status report you could use in the Worked Example section but, however it looks, think of it as being structured into three levels as follows:

Level 1
What is the overall status of each of the projects this week? (It's good to show the status from previous weeks too). Red/Amber/Green ("traffic

light") reporting is probably the easiest way to indicate this. Remember that the phrase "On target" could have up to three dimensions to it – the date the project is due to end, the amount of work (man-days) involved and the budget. Green means you have a plan and you're running to the plan. Amber means you've drifted a bit but you're taking steps to bring things back on track. Red means the plan is gone to hell and the project will have to be replanned.

The only other thing that you might want to put in Level 1 is what you can think of as "I need help". This is where there might be an issue that is outside your control or authority to resolve. Maybe you need help from your boss or other stakeholders to get resources. Or maybe there is some roadblock in the project that you want help in removing because you're unable to do it. Or maybe you need a decision made – you don't care what it is, you just want it made, maybe by the stakeholders.

If this was the case, then you would also put into Level 1:

- What – here's the issue.
- Action – here's what I want done about it.
- Who – who has to do this.
- Deadline – here's when it has to be done by.
- Threat – here's what will happen if it isn't done.

So, for example, you might say, "I need two more project managers by 31st July. My boss is the person who has to get these. If I don't get them, then I won't be able to start the X and Y projects on 1 August". (Nothing like a threat to focus the mind!)

Level 2

What tends to be missing from many status reports is a history of how the project got to be where it is now. If you don't provide a history, stakeholders will provide their own. In general, if this happens, their history will not be favourable to you. So, for instance, supposing a project was meant to finish on 21st September of a particular year and it now looks like finishing on 29th November, what will the stakeholders think or say? Almost certainly, they'll start to talk in terms of "the slip".

So, in order to avoid this scenario, you need to interpret the dates for them. You (and nobody else) needs to write the history and explain how the project got to be where it is. Here's how to do that. (It's described for the date. If you're tracking the budget and/or the work, then you would do it for those as well.) For the date, you would say:

- Here's what it was originally.
- Here's what it is now.
- Here's how it changed. (You would have a line for each time the date changed along with an explanation of when and why it changed.)

Level 3

Finally, in Level 3, you can point your stakeholders at all of the detailed information available about the project.

Send out your status report once a week – probably towards close of business on that week. This chapter talked earlier about RAG reporting but there's also SAS reporting. It stands for "Send and Scarper". So you've got to picture – your status report is there on your screen, your bag is packed, you've got your hat and coat on, the engine of your car is running, you hit "Send", run out the door before anybody has had a chance to read it and switch off your mobile phone and/or Blackberry!

Because, if you've had the projects planned properly, if you've done your tracking prudently, as described above, and reported the status honestly, then your stakeholders can't ask for more than that. After all – you're entitled to a life!

Worked Example

When we last left the Acme company, you may remember they had decided, for definite, to do their top priority projects, numbers 1-8. Here (in Figure 15.1) is what these might look like on a plan that the CEO was using to track these projects. (For clarity, the detailed entries for Work and Budget are only partly filled in.)

Figure 15.1 Project tracking at the organisation level

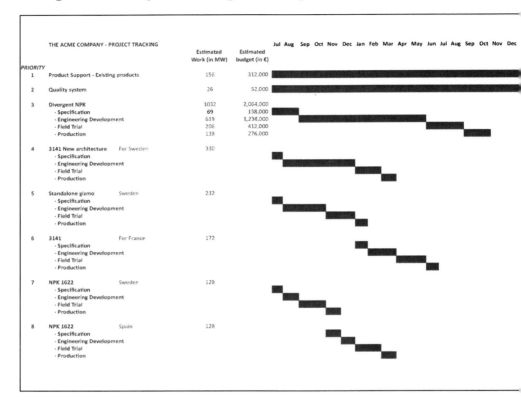

And here (in Figure 15.2) is what it might look like a couple of months later with some of the actuals added

Figure 15.2 Project tracking showing actuals

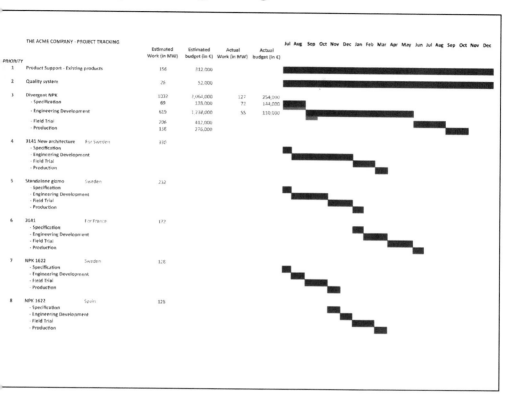

And overleaf (in figure 15.3) is what the weekly status reporting for these projects might look like.

Figure 15.3 Weekly project tracking report

THE ACME COMPANY - PROJECT TRACKING		Project Manager	Estimated Work (in MW)	Estimated budget (in €)	Actual Work (in MW)	Actual budget (in €)	J A S O N D J F M A M J J A S O N D	STATUS	STATUS Green / Blue			Change History	Detailed Plan
PRIORITY									Week1	Week 2	Week 3	Hyperlink	Hyperlink
1	Product Support - Existing products	Charlie	156	312,000				On target	5	5	5		
2	Quality system	Bill	76	52,000				Some problems	3	3	3		
3	Divergent NPK	Fred	1032	2,064,000	127	254,000		Some problems	3	5	5		
	- Specification		69	138,000	72	144,000							
	- Engineering Development		619	1,238,000	55	110,000							
	- Field Trial		206	412,000									
	- Production		138	276,000									
4	3141 New architecture	For Sweden Bjorn	330					On target	5	1	3		
	- Specification												
	- Engineering Development												
	- Field Trial												
	- Production												
5	Standalone gizmo	Sweden Anna	232					On target	5	5	1		
	- Specification												
	- Engineering Development												
	- Field Trial												
	- Production												
6	3141	For France Brigitte	172					No written plan	0	5	1		
	- Specification												
	- Engineering Development												
	- Field Trial												
	- Production												
7	NPK 1642	Sweden Anna	128					On target	5	3	1		
	- Specification												
	- Engineering Development												
	- Field Trial												
	- Production												
8	NPK 1642	Spain Manuel	126					Some problems	3	3	3		
	- Specification												
	- Engineering Development									3.6	4.3	4.3		
	- Field Trial												
	- Production												

This report shows everything that everyone would reasonably want to know:

- This week's overall status is there as well as the historical status, week on week.
- All three dimensions are shown – date, work and budget.
- Both planned and actual are shown.
- If people want to see detailed information, they can follow the hyperlinks to the project's change history or detailed plan.

At-a-glance summary

1. Track the projects every day.
2. Report the status every week.

Chapter 16

Step 8: Get Your Projects Done As Quickly As Possible

If you do everything discussed so far, you can get to a point where all of your projects are running on target. From time to time, you may have problems that will tip them off this status, but you should be able to take action quickly to restore them to Green. The number of fire fights you and your project managers have to deal with will have reduced significantly. There's one more thing you can do to improve this situation even further. You can get the projects done faster and that is the subject of this penultimate chapter.

Why don't we routinely do this anyway? Why don't we try to shorten any project we run? It seems to me that the answer can be found among the following factors:

1. Most project managers don't think it's actually possible. *They* think *they're* lucky if they can bring the project in on time and within budget.
2. The stakeholders don't think it's actually possible – *they* think *they're* lucky if the project comes in on time and within budget.
3. Nobody knows what getting the project done early would mean financially.
4. Projects aren't planned properly – if they're not planned properly they can't possibly be done quickly.
5. Getting projects done quickly is not in the PMI's Project Management Body of Knowledge (PMBOK).

6.   "What's wrong with the way we do things at the moment?" syndrome.
7.   People are afraid that if they try to do the project fast they'll miss something important.

And so the result of all this is that ... they don't try!
  But there are enormous benefits to getting projects done quicker. They include:

●   Reduced costs and money saved.
●   Increased profits.
●   Improved revenues.
●   Improved cash flow.
●   Stealing a march on competitors.
●   Business benefits delivered quicker.
●   The risk of the project running over greatly reduced.
●   Not to mention ... increased team morale, greater job satisfaction and all that good stuff.

So, what follows here then are seven techniques that can be used by your project managers to get their projects done quicker. The only assumption these techniques make is that your organisation is routinely planning and executing its projects properly, i.e. as described in Chapter 6. The techniques are these:

1.   Basic techniques;
2.   Scope and plan a project in a day;
3.   Calculate the value of getting it done early;
4.   Lay the plan out as a strip board.
5.   Do a Mission Briefing for the team and for the other stakeholders.
6.   Make every day count (8 items).
7.   O'Connell's Law,
and they are discussed in turn.

1. Basic Techniques

These are the simplest and most obvious techniques of all. Get your project managers to do the following:

1. Ask people if they could try to get something finished before the weekend, a long weekend, a holiday weekend, a public holiday, their own holidays, Christmas, Easter – irrespective of what the plan actually says.
2. Avoid multi-tasking. If there is any occurrence of multi-tasking on your project focus on trying to get rid of it. Somebody working full-time for you for a month will be more valuable (in terms of speeding up the project) than that same person half-time for two months. You get the same amount of work (1 person-month) from them so that should make it an easy "sell" to their boss.
3. Can you parallel things? Or overlap things, i.e. can you actually start job B – which strictly, speaking depends on job A, before job A finishes? It might be possible. For example, you don't have to wait until all the testing of something is finished before you start fixing the errors in it.
4. The Critical Path is the shortest path through the project. Have a look at the jobs on the Critical Path and see if you can shorten any of them.

2. Scope and Plan a Project in a Day

It is possible to scope and plan a project – even a very large one – in a day. You can be sceptical about this if you like. All I can tell you is that I've done it a lot and it works. If you don't scope and plan the project in a day, what's the alternative? It goes something like this:

1. Somebody identifies some kind of need or requirement or problem that needs to be solved.
2. Based on this, somebody does some ferreting around and then writes a proposal/business case/specification.
3. This is reviewed by the stakeholders and the reviews are fed back to the author of the document.
4. There are updates to the document plus, perhaps, flurries of email exchanges, phone calls, requests for information and meetings to resolve various issues.

5.   Items 3 and 4 get looped around a number of times until finally …
6.   There is agreement on what is going to be done.
7.   Then somebody is charged with building a plan.
8.   That somebody does some ferreting around and then writes a plan.
9.   That plan is reviewed by some or all of the stakeholders and the reviews are fed back to the author.
10. There are updates to the plan, perhaps more emails, phone calls, requests for information and meetings – particularly if there is a gap between what the stakeholders want and what the project team say is possible.
11. Items 9 and 10 get looped around a number of times until finally …
12. There is agreement on the plan.

This process can take weeks … months … years, in some cases.

As an alternative to all of this carry-on, you can scope and plan the project in a day.

In their book, *Developing Products in Half the Time* [7], the authors Smith and Reinertsen refer to the beginning of the project as "the fuzzy front end". They say this:

"Time is an irreplaceable resource. When a month of potential development time is squandered, it can never be recovered … each month of delay has a quantifiable cost of delay. Our goal as developers is to find opportunities to buy cycle time for less than this cost. These opportunities, large and small, appear throughout the development process. There is, however, one place that we could call the 'bargain basement' of cycle time reduction opportunities. It is the place that we consistently find the least expensive opportunities to achieve large improvements in time to market. We call this stage of development the Fuzzy Front End of the development programme. It is the fuzzy zone between when the opportunity is known and when we mount a serious effort on the development project."

If the "fuzzy front end" is where "opportunities to achieve large improvements in time to market" are greatest, then scoping and planning a project in a day is way of maxing out those opportunities.

Projects can often be very start-stop in nature. We do some stuff and then we have to wait, for example, for reviews, or approval or for input from other people. Nowhere is this truer than in the fuzzy front end. Everyone believes they have something to contribute, lots of people want "sign-off" and there are always those who feel that their input is being ignored. At the same time, because the project hasn't really yet gotten off the ground, there are always a million and one things more immediate and pressing. The net result of all of this can be a long and frustrating period while requirements are identified, nailed down and agreed. You can circumvent all of this by concertina-ing them into one decisive, devastatingly effective event called a Project Scoping and Planning Session.

The benefits of this approach are:

- Projects launched in a day. The project is actually running by the end of the day. There is no quicker and more cost-effective way to begin a project.
- Clear project objectives, project requirements and agreement/ buy-in on these from the stakeholders.
- Accurate estimates upon which firm commitments can be made.
- A clear picture of how the project will unfold.
- A kick-start to the project.

For more detail, you can find out exactly how to run such a session in my book *Fast Projects* [6].

3. Calculate the Value of Getting it Done Early

Get your project managers to complete a profit model like the one in Figure 16.1. This will show you pretty quickly what the financial benefit of finishing early would be.

Figure 16.1 shows an example of a simple profit model for a product development project. It shows the cost of developing the product versus the revenues that are projected to be achieved.

Figure 16.1 Profit model for a product development project

All figures in US$
Figures in italics must be entered by the user

		Development				Year 1			
		-Q4	-Q3	-Q2	-Q1	Q1	Q2	Q3	Q4
PRODUCT REVENUES									
Average sales price	350					350	350	350	350
Market size in units						40,000	40,000	50,000	60,000
Market share						20%	25%	25%	25%
Unit sales						8,000	10,000	12,500	15,000
Dollar sales						2,800,000	3,500,000	4,375,000	5,250,000
PRODUCT COSTS									
Unit cost	50					50	50	50	50
Cost of goods sold						400,000	500,000	625,000	750,000
Gross margin in $						2,400,000	3,000,000	3,750,000	4,500,000
Gross margin in %						86%	86%	86%	86%
DEVELOPMENT COSTS									
Cost per team member	100,000	100,000	100,000	100,000	100,000	100,000	100,000	100,000	100,000
Number of team members		2	6	6	4	2	1	0.5	0.5
Development team cost		200,000	600,000	600,000	400,000	200,000	100,000	50,000	50,000
Marketing costs	15%					420,000	525,000	656,250	787,500
General & administrative	5%					140,000	175,000	218,750	262,500
Total costs		200,000	600,000	600,000	400,000	760,000	800,000	925,000	1,100,000
PROFIT / LOSS									
Profit (loss) before tax (PBT)		- 200,000	- 600,000	- 600,000	- 400,000	2,040,000	2,700,000	3,450,000	4,150,000
Cumulative PBT		- 200,000	- 800,000	- 1,400,000	- 1,800,000	240,000	2,940,000	6,390,000	10,540,000

TOTAL PBT	29,940,000

Having built such a model it is possible for the project manager and the stakeholders to examine what the effect of finishing early would be. Could they charge a higher price for their product because it's on the market earlier? As a result could they grab a bigger market share? Could being to market early mean that the product's lifetime will be extended?

So, for example, they could see what the effect would be of:

- shortening the project by three months;
- charging $400 per unit instead of $350;
- assuming a 5% higher market share and an additional quarter's sales, but at reduced volume.

In this example the profit before tax (PBT) would be $29,940,000 for the unshortened project and $30,240,000 for the shortened project – an additional $300,000.

Equally, they could look at the negative scenario. What if the project runs late? What if it ran over by three months? Then the revenues would be delayed by three months and the costs would continue for a further three months. This would cause the PBT to drop from $ 29,940,000 to $ 24,350,000, a loss of over $ 5.5 million! So there would be a big incentive to see that this project wasn't delayed.

4. Lay the Plan Out as a Strip Board

Here's an idea taken from the movie-making industry where people are good at running projects. Movie people routinely deliver large, expensive projects that are part-art, part-science on time, within budget to a very high degree of quality. The key to doing this is that the plans to shoot a movie are broken down to the *1-day* level of detail (as opposed to the 1-5 days described in Chapter 5).

Movie-makers do this using a tool that is known as a "strip board". Think of a strip board as a giant spreadsheet. The rows of the spreadsheet are the days of the shoot. The first series of columns in the spreadsheet list all of the cast members – from the highest paid star to the lowest walk-on part. The remaining columns list all of the other things – props, special effects, animals, special services, equipment and so on – required to shoot on that particular day. Months before a movie is due to be shot, somebody goes through the script (the definition of the goal) and creates a strip board for the movie. The strip board essentially shows what every member of the team is doing every day of the project. Get the idea?

So if you want to get your project done:

- in the shortest possible time;
- as cheaply as possible;
- with the minimum of delays and waste.

get your project managers to plan it down to the day level of detail and document it on a strip board. There's an example of a piece of a strip board shown in Figure 16.2.

Figure 16.2 Example of a piece of a strip board

Day #		Date	Cast (Jobs)									
			Charlie	Engineer #2	Engineer #3	Engineer #4	Technical author	Marketing people (3)	Admin Assistant	Tester #1	Tester #2	Project Management
1	1	09-Jan-07	Project	Project	Project	Project	Project	Project kic	Project ki	Project	Project	Project kickoff
	2	10-Jan-07	6 Gathe									236 Project management [up to 1/2 day]
	3	11-Jan-07	9 Prepare user questionnaires									236 Project management [up to 1/2 day]
	4	12-Jan-07	9 Prepare user questionnaires						10 Distribute user question			236 Project management [up to 1/2 day]
2	5	15-Jan-07	7 Review with Marketing					7 Review	11 Retrieve questionnaires			236 Project management [up to 1/2 day]
	6	16-Jan-07	12 Analyse information									236 Project management [up to 1/2 day]
	7	17-Jan-07	13 Write requirements document									236 Project management [up to 1/2 day]
	8	18-Jan-07	13 Write requirements document									236 Project management [up to 1/2 day]
	9	19-Jan-07	13 Write requirements document									236 Project management [up to 1/2 day]
3	10	22-Jan-07	13 Write requirements document									236 Project management [up to 1/2 day]
	11	23-Jan-07	13 Write requirements document									236 Project management [up to 1/2 day]
	12	24-Jan-07	13 Write requirements document									236 Project management [up to 1/2 day]
	13	25-Jan-07	13 Write requirements document									236 Project management [up to 1/2 day]
	14	26-Jan-07	13 Write requirements document									236 Project management [up to 1/2 day]
4	15	29-Jan-07	13 Write requirements document						15 Circulate document			236 Project management [up to 1/2 day]
	16	30-Jan-07	17,18 Review meeting / changes to docume				16, 17 Individual review [1/2 day each					236 Project management [up to 1/2 day]
	17	31-Jan-07	18 Changes to document									236 Project management [up to 1/2 day]
	18	01-Feb-07	18,19 Changes to document (inc. circulate again)									236 Project management [up to 1/2 day]
	19	02-Feb-07	20-22 Second review / Signoff / Reqs compl				20-22 Sec	20-22 Second review / Sig				236 Project management [up to 1/2 day]

5. Do a Mission Briefing for the Team and for the Stakeholders

A mission briefing is where your project manager takes the team through the project plan line by line, asking them to look for opportunities to shorten the project. It is almost inevitable that they will come up with some. This could also be done with the stakeholders, asking them to do the same.

6. Make Every Day Count

You can make every day count by getting your project managers to get their teams to do the following:

1.   Don't do it tomorrow if it can be done today. Encourage an attitude of "can I finish this today?"

2. Encourage everybody to be hypersensitive to changes that increase the scope of the project.
3. If team members find themselves waiting for somebody else, get them to raise an alert.
4. If team members are aware of a potential delay coming up, flag it as soon as it's known.
5. Keep Dance Cards up-to-date. This way people will know if they've over allocated themselves. Better still, use the Dance Card to avoid over allocating themselves in the first place.
6. If team members can start a job early, do so.
7. If they can finish a job early without compromising quality, do so.
8. If a piece of the project can be delivered using a simpler or quicker approach, then do so.

7. O'Connell's Law

It's not a particularly common phenomenon but when it happens it's glorious. For want of a better name I have called it O'Connell's Law. It says that once a team finds itself ahead of schedule it will try to get even more ahead of schedule. So, if you can once get ahead of schedule, you get a snowball effect. The team want to pull ahead even further. If you can once get some traction, using any of the techniques described above, you will find that the chances of your project coming in early increase enormously.

At-a-glance summary
Run your projects as quickly as possible using the following techniques:

1. Basic techniques.
2. Scope and plan a project in a day.
3. Calculate the value of getting it done early.
4. Lay the plan out as a strip board.
5. Do a Mission Briefing for the team and for the other stakeholders.
6. Make every day count (8 items).
7. O'Connell's Law.

Chapter 17

What You've Achieved II

If you've done the work described in the last three chapters, then your organisation should be humming along nicely. Let's look again at the sources of big waste that we spoke about in Chapter 2.

1. **There is waste every time you switch people between projects**
    This was dealt with in Part 2.

2. **There is waste every time you don't plan a project properly**
    Now you're planning all projects properly. Problem solved.

3. **There is waste every time you have to deal with a fire fight**
    There are still fire fights – and there always will be. But the way you are running projects now means that the fire fights that occur will only be those which genuinely could not have been anticipated.

4. **There is waste because people are working long hours**
    They're not! Working long hours will have become and will continue to be something of a rarity. Problem solved.

5. **There is waste every time a project goes astray or is cancelled.**
    Because of the quality of the planning it will be unusual for projects to go astray or have to be cancelled. (Projects may still get cancelled because the business case for them has changed but that's a separate issue.)

6.   There is waste because morale goes down
Morale should be high in this new scheme of things.

7.   There is waste due to multi-tasking
You have essentially stopped multi-tasking. Problem solved.

So now, here's what things look like. Not bad for a few week's work.

Cause of Waste	Dealt with in Part 2
8.Switching people between projects	Yes
9.Not planning projects properly	Yes
10.Having to deal with fire fights	As much as is possible
11.Working long hours	Yes
12.Projects going astray or being cancelled	Yes
13.Morale going down	Yes
14.Multitasking	Yes

Bibliography

1. DeMarco, Tom. *The Deadline: A Novel About Project Management.* New York: Dorset House Publishing, 1997.

2. Brookes, Frederick P. *The Mythical Man Month and Other Essays on Software Engineering.* Addison Wesley, 1995.

3. O'Connell, Fergus. *How to Run Successful Projects III – The Silver Bullet.* London: Addison Wesley, 2001.

4. Yourdon, Edward, *Death March (Second edition).* New Jersey: Prentice Hall, 2003.

5. Leach, Lawrence P., *Critical Chain Project Management (2nd edition).* Boston: Artech House, 2004.

6. O'Connell, Fergus. *Fast Projects: Project Management When Time is Short.* London: Prentice Hall, 2007.

7. Smith, Preston G. & Reinertsen, Donald G., *Developing Products in Half The Time: New Rules, New Tools.* New York: Wiley, 1997.

Lightning Source UK Ltd.
Milton Keynes UK
172696UK00001B/15/P